To Laura,

W9-CFJ-069

Defeating Breast Cancer Organically

Best health

Laura

Joe and Laura Patrina

Defeating Breast Cancer Organically

To order additional copies of this book:
www.amazon.com
www.barnesandnoble.com

Published in the United States of America

ISBN *hardcover: 9781948000048*
ISBN *softcover: 9781948000055*

The Authors

Joe & Laura Patrina, parents of four, live in Connecticut.

Laura's Note – 2018

Four years ago I was diagnosed with breast cancer tumors.

Once Joe and I decided to tackle the tumors using organic, self-healing methods, our children urged Joe to keep a journal of everything being researched, every medical meeting and every element of the organic protocol under assembly.

A year later, with the tumors no longer appearing on the Mammogram, women young and old soon contact us looking for information.

Joe compiles his journal and research notes, organizing them into a manuscript titled, "*Defeating Breast Cancer*. He continues taking notes for the second, third and forth years as well, as we go for exams with a sonogram expert in New York City.

Defeating Breast Cancer speaks unfiltered. The ideas and decisions prevailing over the course of four years – even the "far out" ones - are reflected just as experienced.

Laura Patrina

Joe's Note – 2018

Back in 2014, medical professionals diagnosed my wife Laura with Stage 1 breast cancer. A year or so prior, Angelina Jolie, an American icon, ordered both of her breasts removed as a precaution!

At the time, Angelina showed no signs of breast cancer, but medical professionals told her that, similar to her relatives, she possessed the genetic probability to develop it based upon BRCA testing, described later.

As I write this firsthand account, many American women are jumping off gangplanks simply upon hearing the words "breast cancer," with brutal surgery becoming the response du jour once the words are uttered. Well, Laura and I assumed that we, too, would head down the surgery/radiation/chemotherapy road.

Yet, at the same time, we knew we could explore another "self-healing" fork, a path that directs and organizes the body to first deprive, and then kill the cancer, removing both cancer's causes and dependencies, so that the cancer goes away and does not easily return.

Part of this book describes that self-healing path, but the book also depicts how we – Laura, and I – found the courage to actively place our faith in it.

As you will read, three principle rails traverse the path of self-healing: 1) *diet*, i.e., deprive the cancer, as it needs 15 times as much sugar as do normal cells, 2) immune system *empowerment*, free it from its struggle with toxins. And 3), *infiltration*: "trick" cancer into ingesting the very compounds that degrade it. I describe all three assaults, in detail, herein.

Most importantly, I wrote this book for women (and men) who seek to understand the biological foundations that enable these three coordinated rails to exert so much power over the rogue cancer breakout.

As of this writing, a combination of the *Self-Healing Protocol* and Laura's discipline to "follow it to a 'T,'" delivered the results we hoped for.

After three months, Laura's tumors shrank by 50 percent, without surgery, radiation, or chemotherapy.

Five months later, we checked in and the tumors halved once again. Four months after that, no more tumors. It took us one year… to declare a guarded victory, and a second, third and forth year to be sure as we had periodic sonogram and mammogram tests along the way.

I would not have documented *Defeating Breast Cancer* except for the encouragement – a direct command actually – from my second daughter, Tara, aged 19, who insisted: *You better start writing it all down… before you forget it.*

I brushed Tara's "suggestion" aside, saying, *No one wants someone else "telling them" how to do things.*

Her response *Well if you reach just one woman, and you help her, isn't that worth the effort?*

I hope you are that woman.

JA Patrina, 2018

Contents

Getting Started – Highlights

This 270-page book, *"Defeating Breast Cancer – Organically – No Radiation, No Chemotherapy and No Surgery"*, was written in journal form, a retelling of a four-year journey that uncovered the *Self-Healing* protocol described herein.

To give the reader a feel for the tactics of this naturopath approach, "Getting Started" summarizes some of the key elements of the protocol. But while reading "Getting Started" consider the following:

1. Many subtle protocol elements described within the body of this book are not mentioned in "Getting Started", but more, the reasons things work are only described inside the book's pages. Plus, in the journal, you will read about what Laura and I went through within the world of traditional medicine, so as not to be shocked when similar things happen to you.

2. Cancer will not be eliminated by ingesting the abbreviated list of supplements described below; one eliminates cancer by total intellectual immersion into one's biological system, understanding and doing many, many small things that collectively tip the scales againwst the renegade cancer cells.

3. One is not a victim of cancer. Cancer is simply a malfunction within, and needs to be arrested within, hence one needs to know the details of what is going on inside the body. No hand wringing.

4. Alternatively, one can do the opposite, outsource the problem to Radiologists, Oncologists and Surgeons, who kill cancer cells via physical intervention, with noted collateral, often permanent damage, and without any improvement of the body's defensive systems going forward.

5. One should not stumble into decisions on how to eliminate one's cancer. One should know all one can, hence this book, which describes some of the know-how coming from the naturopath side of the equation.

And so, with the "read the whole book" advise just said, let's get started by touching upon the three key topics of the book: *Diet, Infiltration and Empowerment.*

Diet - You Will Learn About Starving Cancer, and That Cancer Craves Sugar

The expanded explanation of "Cancer Craves Sugar" is found in the body of this book. Here we will simply say that healthy cells create energy by combining oxygen and sugar, called *oxidation,* like burning logs on a fire, whereas cancer cells hide from oxygen and instead create their energy by *fermenting* large quantities of sugar, like in a whisky still.

Cancer cells require 16 times as much sugar than normal cells to achieve this.

The diet centerpiece for defeating cancer seeks to provide the body with just enough sugar for healthy cells, while leaving cancer tumors high and dry.

The day one starts with such a diet is the day the cancer cells begin to go hungry. As the weeks go by, and the body's sugar reserves dwindle, tumor cells slowly die of starvation.

You Will Learn How to Poison Cancer and Boost Your Immune System.

Eventually the tumor itself fizzles out, and the time needed for this milestone depends upon the size of the tumor, complemented by the use of *infiltration* "poisoning" tactics that further weaken the nutrient-deprived tumor, and the *empowerment* of one's immune system to help kill off the weakened tumor cells in an accelerated manner.

You Will Learn That Cancer Hates Alkaline Blood

Alkaline blood allows for optimum levels of oxygen transported to the cells, a healthy condition. Conversely, cancer cells shun oxygen and instead ferment sugars, preferring an acidic/low oxygen blood environment.

So, in order to deprive cancer cells, in addition to controlling sugars, one must gravitate to foods that result in greater blood alkalinity.

Note: the foods themselves are not acidic; acidic blood stems from the stomach generating acid to break down incoming food. Foods, such as a steak, require large amounts of stomach acid to break down the steak proteins and fat, with some of this acidic overload entering one's bloodstream.

Conversely, watermelon requires almost no acid, and hence watermelon offers alkalinity as it's digested nutrients make their way into the blood system.

The matrix of sugar/acidic foods versus non-sugar/alkaline foods is presented in the main body of the book.

You Will Learn of the Diabetes and Cancer Connection

As explained later in the book, diabetes – excess sugar in the blood – is an aid to cancer tumors, as extended blood sugar durations give cancer ample time to extract all the sugar they need from the blood stream.

And so, besides dealing with cancer, one simultaneously needs to deal with diabetes. Both ailments involve bodily processes weakened by age, but one can offset the weaknesses via supplementation.

For example, to address diabetic influences on cancer, the book describes a self-run clinical test of a supplement called *Glucose Reduce*, a capsule containing plant extracts known to offset the two causes of diabetes.

There are many other diet related tactics to know not included in this summary. Let's move to *Infiltration*.

You Will Learn About Poisons and Supplements That Disrupt Cancer Cell Division

As one works to get their Diet under control - to deprive cancer of its 16X sugar lifeline – simultaneously, one should introduce infiltration tactics to disrupt cancer's cell division rates.

1. CBD Oil – With Frankincense & Cumin Seed Infusions

Immune system cells are programmed to attack "foreigners" – viruses, bacteria, parasites, funguses as well as sick cells (like cancer cells). Various specialized immune system cells work collectively to identify foreigners, remember foreigners should they return, and kill rampaging foreigners. The different immune cell roles are described in the body of this book.

Cancer cells, part of the host body, are often difficult to detect; technically they are host cells gone astray, not outside foreign invaders. With cancer, one can help the immune system identify these insiders as "bad guy" targets. This is where CBD Oil comes into play.

CBD Oil comes from Hemp plants. The oil attaches to tumor cell wall receptors making the tumor visible to the immune cells so that immune agents attack the now visible tumor as a foreigner. CBD Oil does not stick to the normal cells with normal receptors, hence the cancer cells are specifically "outed".

With the *Bluebird* CBD oil brand we use, Frankincense and Cumin Seed Oils are mixed into the CBD Oil as stealth agents, designed to infiltrate tumors already clinging to the CBD molecules.

Frankincense – the resin from the Boswellia tree - seeps into the tumor, confounding each cancer cell's propensity to divide, arresting the tumor's growth rate, thus providing time for the immune cells to whittle down the tumor.

Black Cumin Oil - derived from black seeds harvested from dessert plants - contains hundreds of organic molecules that our bodies crave. This impressive range of molecules trigger all sorts of benefits, including stimulating the immune system, jumping it into high gear to sort out and destroy foreigners.

Black Cumin also helps with diabetes, so additional Black Cumin supplementation may be appropriate to siphon off the cancer-feeding sugar supplies lingering in the blood stream.

Likewise, besides the Frankincense infused within the CBD oil, stand-alone Frankincense oil can be applied topically at the tumor's surface location, letting the skin deliver the oil's molecules to the area surrounding the tumor.

2. Honey or Maple Syrup Laced with Baking Soda

Foods that help with alkalinity are discussed in the book's Diet section. Here we use food – honey and maple syrup - to trick cancer – a Trojan Horse tactic.

Baking Soda is extremely alkaline and can be added to either Honey or Maple Syrup, then heated up to attach the Baking Soda molecules to the Honey/Maple Sugar molecules.

One ingests the combined mixture, allowing the sugar-starved cancer tumors to vigorously ingest the sugar (similar to a Pet Scan application); the tumors inadvertently ingest high concentrates of alkaline-based baking soda in the process, a substance they detest.

The formula is described in the book.

3. Green Tea Supplements

The book explains that cancer cell receptors only listen for "divide" signals broadcast by one's hormonal system; "die" signals are not heard. To address this, cancer receptors need to be "plugged" to prevent divide signals from reaching the cancer cell's nucleus – don't let cancer hear anything!

A compound in green tea fits nicely in the cancer cells' ENOX2 hormone receptor "antenna", thereby blocking incoming stimulus.

Green tea concentrate can be ingested in capsule form to plug these receptors. However, the plug is water soluble, washing out after four hours. Hence a green tea pill is required every four hours.

Capsol-T produces this supplement, and it includes a slow release nighttime version to keep cancer cells plugged even while you sleep. This amazing phenomenon is described in detail within the book.

You Will Learn How to Empower Your Immune System to Aggressively Attack Your Tumors

Now that we have starved and then tricked the cancer tumors with self-inflicted poisons and hormonal plugs, it is time for the "coup de grace", the execution of diminished cells. The executioners are various immune system cells – all described in detail within the body of this book. We want to provision the immune cells, elevating them to "green beret" levels, in order to maximize their destruction resolve against the renegade cancer cells lurking in the body.

The supplements described below stimulate and feed immune cells.

1. Red Reishi Mushroom Extract – The Stimulant

This extract comes from Red Reishi Mushrooms, originally found in Japan. The organic molecules from the mushroom "heal" imbalances throughout the body, allowing, for example, the liver to operate without stress and constraints.

Likewise, Red Reishi optimizes the creation of immune cells – within the bone marrow and the thalamus gland – to propagate aggressive immune cells.

Besides getting the body to operate effectively, there are claims that certain Reishi molecules actually harm tumor cells.

Historically, Red Reishi is the most cherished medicinal supplement in the orient. It is not a drug going after a particular disease; it is a "wellness" supplement, provisioning the body to do its own bidding.

2. Beta Glucan – Immune Cell Vitamins

Beta Glucans are organic molecules found in many plants that happen to be essential vitamins for immune cells. If diet alone does not yield sufficient levels of glucans, then the immune cells become sluggish. On the other hand, if one carries too much beta glucan in the blood stream, it is simply washed out by the kidney/liver functions.

Hence, especially as one ages, it behooves you to take a daily dose of glucans, just as you would take vitamin C. Both vitamins are water soluble, flushed out of the system daily, requiring replenishment. Glucans are food for immune cells ... feed them.

3. Resveratrol – Opening Capillaries

Resveratrol pills come from red grape skins. These organic molecules relax the circulatory pathways, lowering stress on the heart, and enabling better transport of oxygen, nutrients and immune cells throughout the body.

But You Need to Read the Actual Journal to Cross the Finish Line

Ok, that is a high level look at what is to come inside the book. "Getting Started" did not touch upon the book's other cancer defeating protocol elements, such as energy boosters, oxygen boosters, sleep and stress reducing factors, dental hygiene considerations, inflammation elimination, and body-wide detoxification programs.

So become a student! Read the book's journal details before signing up for invasive medical procedures that ignore these considerations. Some cancer doctors will dismiss all of this as "non-sense", others will patronize you, saying "it can't hurt", and some will say they welcome naturopath assistance "to ease the effect of radiation and/or chemotherapy".

But none will encourage you try an all-out naturopath protocol for 10 - 12 weeks to see if it shrinks your tumors, thereby dodging the need for Radiation, Chemotherapy and Surgery all together.

Decide for yourself.

Get Motivated!

What I document in this book, admittedly, recommends a difficult-to-stick-to protocol dealing with sugars, toxins, and energy levels, but one I believe to be far superior to the short-term "survival statistics" proffered by cancer researchers, pharmaceutical manufacturers, surgeons, radiologists, and oncologists.

These medical interventionists propose surgery, chemotherapy, and radiation as the central options for cure, and they frame success only in terms of improved five-year survival rates.

The chart below, published by the Cancer Treatment Centers of America (CTCA), shows the typical cancer survival presentation for a group of 323 metastatic breast cancer patients who were diagnosed between 2000 and 2011. Each patient in the group was first diagnosed at CTCA and/or received at least part of their initial course of treatment at CTCA.

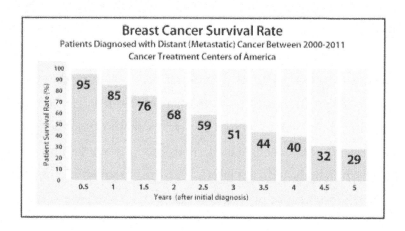

Of the metastatic breast cancer patients shown above, the estimated survival rate at year 5 was 29%. This means that five years after their diagnosis, 29% of the patients in this group were still living. Most probably, had the patients done nothing, most would have died earlier. Treatment did work to some degree.

Conversely, the payoff for pursuing *self-healing* proves immeasurable. Not only will you blunt cancer without assaults on your body, but also you will emerge from *The Self-Healing Protocol* in the best condition imaginable, possibly the best of your life – at an ideal weight, with full energy, and with optimal skin and muscle tone for your age.

You will have started "sick," and ended up — as the saying goes, "Better than Ever", with time itself no longer an eminent threat, and you, yourself in control.

Along the way, as you monitor the shrinkage of your cancer with periodic measurements, reassured that the *Self-Healing Protocol* works for you, your personal health status will be the only statistic that matters, not the statistics of others. Yet, due to the protocol's complexity, the need to overcome food addictions, and the persistent time commitment, the *Self-Healing Protocol* may not work for everyone. It requires you to assume the role of an action hero fighting for your own results, whereas standard medicine allows you to remain passive, weakening your body and psyche with surgical and needle incisions, and weakening every cell in your body with radiation and drug bombardments that ignore the root cause of your condition.

Some, even after reading this book and accepting all or most of it, will find the *Self-Healing Protocol* too tedious and instead will opt for brutal surgery/radiation/chemo solutions, hoping to gain whatever life-extension potentials these protocols offer.

At my age, you might reason, *standard medicine* (such as it is), *offers the only bet I can tolerate, anyway.*

By reading this book, you will discover which bet suits your orientation: brutal medical intervention or extended personal discipline.

No, there's no "Get Out of Jail Free" card in *this* game.

Most of the women with whom I have spoken claim that they have the discipline to implement the protocol... and I believe most do.

But be mindful. You *can* elect to do both. Even if you go with medical intervention, you can still adopt all or part of the *Self-Healing Protocol*, before and after medical intervention, to test and strengthen your body.

Least one guesses that the *Self-Healing Protocol* only works for early-stage cancer, the leverage actually favors the later stage of the disease, although, admittedly, at some point, nothing can save you, once the disease becomes overwhelming.

Consider this: Prior to reaching the point of no return, over-expanded cancer colonies depend completely upon the fixed, moment-by-moment nutritional resources the blood stream offers, and are therefore more easily deprived through dietary measures.

And once *diet* deprives cancer cells and they become increasingly impotent — the billions of *empowered* immune system cells the body musters every second can tip the scales, bringing death and destruction to the weakened enemy, day and night. More developed cancer may take longer to wear down, but it remains vulnerable.

And do not forget the *infiltration* tactics, where things cancer tumors hate can directly assail them without hurting the body… things such as heat, common baking soda, oxygen, green tea, saffron and even frankincense (specifics described later).

Until now, your cancer resided on "Easy Street," never facing all three frontal assaults.

You have never deprived it of sugar, even for a moment; your immune system never launched an "all-out" attack, and certainly natural poisons never infiltrated it, making *it* feel sick itself every second of its existence.

Through *Diet, Empowerment* and *Infiltration,* the *Self-Healing Protocol* could turn *your* body into a medical powerhouse, designed to eliminate both current and future rogue cancer cells.

The Tiny World of Cellular Biology Proves the Key

This book also details specific theories of what causes a normal cell to turn cancerous, although strictly speaking, the root cause is immaterial; as regardless of cause, the book's protocol simply works.

But every serious person ponders, "What is the actual cause?" ... So why not explore the possibilities?

I propose that viruses, "ninja-like" parasites, infiltrate normal but enfeebled cells, and take them over at the DNA level, flipping genetic switches, turning them cancerous.

Some dismiss this "viral" explanation as "not proven." They instead believe that *risk factors*, such as cigarette toxins, cause *spontaneous genetic mutations*, which turn healthy cells into cancer *during cell division* – yet they provide no further details on how such "spontaneity" takes place so consistently from person-to-person.

At any rate, prepare yourself to contemplate the root cause topic to gain a deeper look into the world of cellular biology at the conceptual level.

Note: as the author, I aspire for the reader to understand the immensity of our biological system without employing cryptic language. The medical world has its own necessary system of words with specific meanings, essential for doctors to communicate precisely amongst themselves.

But technical terminology inadvertently shuts the layperson out of the dialogue. This book describes cellular biology in conceptual terms, giving the reader a better chance to visualize the cancer battlefield.

Economics Is Insidious

Most cancer doctors will not initiate discussion of biological subjects, as they do not, for a minute, believe that you can or should understand them. Rather than engaging you with cause-and-effect concepts, cancer doctors merely offer patients Door #1 and Door #2 treatment options in a most perfunctory manner, citing survival rates.

Doctors only delve into deeper conversations with other doctors who have endured the medical school gauntlet... and doctors believe in themselves absolutely and wholeheartedly.

They embody "real science," employing the best techniques and procedures possible. Everything else remains dangerous fantasy, proposed by wishful amateurs, with no data to hang their hopes upon.

Most doctors fall victim to the data-driven doctrines molded at the medical schools of their youth - which all deal with the statistical outcome of intervention methods like chemo, radiation and surgery. And once in practice, they stay on this track, reinforced by the conformist thinking of their esteemed colleagues ... so much so that they cannot dare to proffer non-intervention, non-statistical self-healing possibilities.

Moreover, doctors do not sell "alternative solutions". The old expression "Follow the money" dominates the field of cancer like most other businesses. Cancer medicine revenues flow from surgery, radiation, chemotherapy, charities and research... *period!*

But the money angle runs even deeper.

No matter how cancer doctors personally feel about alternative cures, they have no choice but to keep quiet, as they risk litigation if, for example, they recommend the *Self-Healing Protocol* and the patient only follows it half-heartedly and fails.

Additionally, the American Medical Association discredits any doctor who strays from the medical profession's sanctioned treatments.

Mainly, insurance companies drive the market, paying only for treatments sanctioned by mysterious medical-bishops who have the final say in how much society will pay... and for what.

These vast, powerful economic forces have nothing to do with your best interests, and, I'm sorry to say, you must keep the medical industry's intellectual prejudices and economic motivations top-of-mind at all times when interacting with a "medical professional."

For the record, Laura did not oppose surgery, chemotherapy, or radiation, per se, and would willingly employ these if her self-healing attempt did not reverse or at least arrest her condition in the three-month time frame we set to try all of this.

To be clear, Laura and I oppose *the positioning* of surgery, chemotherapy, and radiation as the *centerpiece* game in town, a "one-party system" not open to challenge, using fear to herd in frightened patients.

An example: Some hospitals now offer three weeks of intense radiation rather than six weeks of standard radiation, boasting that they are years ahead of the others. Their pitch: "*Would you rather go through 30 radiation treatments? Or half that?*" These are false choices, as they never mention "*How about none?*"

Self-directed Independence

In contrast, *Defeating Breast Cancer* is a connect-the-dots book, which relies on biological forces that you can harness on your own, rather than falling victim to the statistically justified, economic interests of others.

After reading this account, you will enjoy far superior conversations with any doctor, nutritionist, or specialist you consult regarding causes and cures.

And if what they claim does not ring true, you continue on your own way without fear.

Enough said. Now let's get to the good news: the results!

In one year's time, Laura's cancer tumors were no longer visible on the mammogram, and Laura sparkled with energy and vitality. We next entered our "Trust, but Verify" years of watching her health closely, using semi-annual 3D sonograms to examine Laura's breast and lymph tissue. So, as they say, "It's all good," but still I expect that you, the reader, will insist upon further encouragement beyond mere claims of success.

Therefore, I wrote *Defeating Breast Cancer* in story form so that the reader can discover and accumulate *know-how and courage* the way we did... one nugget at a time.

We know of more than 100 different types of cancer. The *Self-Healing Protocol,* described herein, worked for one person and for one type of breast cancer cell. I often wonder if the protocol works well specifically with tumor-based cancers and not, for instance, with blood cancers.

Nevertheless, regardless of your cancer type, start with this document as the basis for obtaining a general, "plain speaking" understanding of cellular biology, of the immune system, of digestion, of toxicity, of acidic-versus-alkaline blood, of "free radicals," of energy, of oxygen, and of the cause and treatment of cancer.

From this point of origin, you begin. You must dig, through research and through interaction with health specialists and cancer survivors, to fine-tune a precision protocol that counters your cancer's specific idiosyncrasies. It is a journey *home.*

Grit and Grace

At some point along our self-healing yellow brick road, Laura decreed that I made a good *medical concierge,* the one deciphering the strategies, making the phone calls, ordering the supplements, and chauffeuring her on all the highway driving. I became "The Wizard's Scarecrow" with his diploma, and yes, in the end, my research-fed ideas proved worthy.

But it was Laura's iron discipline in the early, unproven moments that proved amazing. Once she got the gist of the latest find, Laura ("Dorothy," if you will) would devour it, folding one more new practice into an evolving, overall cancer-defeating protocol.

Yes, fear would descend at times, but Laura would push back, rejoining the hunt again… and again.

By the way, the total cost of defeating Laura's breast cancer came to less than $15,000. Whereas a single day in a hospital runs $8,000. I will ponder this, too, later in the book.

This Is *NOT* A "…For Dummies" Book

Ok, we've got a lot to cover. Some advisors suggest that I cut certain sections of the book possibly too detailed for the average reader, such as *free radical biochemical chain reactions,* or about *the digestion of sugars and fats,* or on extrapolating *the properties of energy*, or on *the role of immune system* cells, etc.

They propose I write a book simply listing the cancer-fighting rules one should follow and be done with it.

I reject the "For Dummies" approach, because most of the people with whom I conversed while writing wanted to know the "*why's, how's and what's…*" behind the step-by step procedures in a cancer-cure rulebook.

Medically, the protocol worked, and by exploring the science and the theories behind it, you, too, get to weigh in with your own thoughts on the complete set of causes and effects proposed herein.

The one thing I can assure you of is this: understanding the body's biochemical/energy design will give you the confidence you need to fend off cancer yourself.

Indeed, knowledge *is* power.

PART I
MEETING CANCER

Chapter 1 – The Phone Call

Laura got the phone call. She was diagnosed with Stage "1A" Breast Cancer. For some reason, she waited all day to tell me.

The mammogram reveals two tumors in her right breast: a larger, nine-millimeter node (the size of a pencil eraser) at 3 o'clock, and a smaller four-millimeter node below it, at around 5 o'clock. The relatively small tumor sizes draw the Stage 1 rating (Stages 1-4 are described below).

Discovered by way of mammogram and verified a few days later by a powerful sonogram, both tumors are biopsied with a needle designed to clip a piece of flesh so that the local pathology lab can determine the specific tumor cell type.

The biopsy procedure also places two tiny titanium markers inside of the breast next to the tumor nodes to easily locate them in the future.

I felt uneasy about the biopsy, as I thought for certain the needle procedure would break off many tumor cells, allowing them to spread. At the time, I said nothing.

There are three main types of breast cancer cells, with Laura's the most common. Referred to as estrogen-sensitive breast cancer, this cell type is found in 70 percent of breast cancer cases.

Laura gets a second phone call from her gynecologist when the pathology department at Hartford Hospital in Connecticut positively identified the cancer cell type as estrogen-sensitive. The hospital keeps the biopsied tissue on file at the lab, in the event other doctors want to examine it.

The Different Types of Breast Cancer:

• *Estrogen and/or Progesterone Sensitive*: 70 percent of breast cancers "grow in response" to the hormone estrogen, and about 65 percent of these also "grow in response" to the hormone, progesterone. These hormones, which fluctuate in intensity with the menstrual cycle, do not cause the cancer; they instead urge the cancer to multiply, i.e., to "grow in response" on a cyclical basis (more on this later).

• *HER2 Positive:* 20 percent of breast cancers are HER2 positive, where having too many copies of the HER2 gene in one's DNA causes the production of high levels of the HER2 protein inside the cell. Similar to estrogen (described above), the HER2 proteins tell cells to grow and divide, **but because HER2 is always present, i.e., non-cyclical, HER2 breast cancer often proves more aggressive.**

• *Triple Negative*: an extremely aggressive form of breast cancer, unrelated to 1) estrogen, 2) progesterone, or 3) HER2 factors … hence the "Triple Negative" moniker. Approximately 10 percent of Breast Cancer cases are "Triple Negative," and they are the worst for reasons I could not uncover (maybe the cancer profession only knows what this cancer is *not* – it is *not* estrogen, progesterone, or HER2 driven).

A few days later Laura and I meet with a recommended breast cancer surgeon at Hartford Hospital who, with a magic marker, draws us a sketch of a human breast on the sheet of paper covering the examination table.

He lays out but two options: 1) a lumpectomy (cut the tumors out, and cut a few related lymph nodes out as well) and then radiate both the right breast and the remaining right arm pit lymph nodes for 50 days, or option 2) a full mastectomy of the right breast and arm pit lymph nodes, with no radiation required (nothing left to radiate).

I stand aghast at this whole nonchalant presentation.

The lymph nodes, by the way, are removed in case some of the cancer tumor cells have drifted from the tumor to a near-by lymph gland via the lymphatic system. The possibility that escaped cancer cells sat trapped in the 3 or 4 breast-drainage lymph nodes was cited as a serious concern.

The lymphatic system is a separate system from the blood system, with its own vessels that, among other jobs, drain dying cells and transport immune cells (more on this later).

I interject that I oppose removing the arm pit lymph nodes, as this impinges the lymphatic pathway out of the arm and chest cavity for on-going lymphatic vessel needs, and that loss of nodes can lead to swollen arms and other permanent effects due to the lymph vessels incurring scarring and blockage from the surgery.

The surgeon brushes off my worries about surgically removed lymph nodes, and goes on to present survival statistics for his two procedural options – lumpectomy and full mastectomy – confidently proclaiming the improved life expectancy rate of each out to <u>five</u> years.

I know a few women, 60 to 80+ years old, who have survived breast cancer. Ultimately, they had unwittingly chosen both alternatives. The problem? Over the long term, it always ended up in a double mastectomy:

1. The first breast cancer occurrence would be treated by lumpectomy/radiation and the patient would be good for a number of years.

2. Then the second breast would become infected in, say, Year Eight, again treated by lumpectomy/radiation.

3. Then, by Year Fourteen, the original breast became infected again, this time requiring a mastectomy, <u>as you cannot use radiation a second time.</u>

4. Finally the second breast, too, would again become infected, leading to the final double mastectomy.

5. Even after double mastectomy, where there is no breast tissue left, the cancer still can resurface by metastasizing into a different cell type, such as lung or bone cancer.

In the cases of which I am aware, the root cause of the cancer was never discussed let alone treated, so the cancer – probably never completely eradicated - just kept coming back. Laura, at 50 years old and the mother of four, wanted to go another 30-to-40 years if possible, and all of this talk about 5-year survival horizons flabbergasted us.

Beside bringing up gruesome long-term survivor stories like these, I also tell the doctor that I had direct experience with cancer due to the death of my first wife, some 30 years ago. He grimaces, knowing what was to come, but I tell the story anyway.

In the late 1980's, my first wife, Janna, succumbed to Hodgkin's lymphoma (a blood cancer) after an 11-year fight.

We had embraced the whole chemo/radiation/surgery program to the hilt at places like Sloan Kettering and Mount Sinai in NYC, until the end, when doctors finally said she had but one week to live. Only then did I muster the guts to start her on the macrobiotic cancer diet (a Japanese vegetarian diet) I had been studying for a year.

The day I brought her home, I hired two cooks to prepare the macrobiotic vegetarian-based meals. A week later she was stable. A month later she was out of her wheelchair, going for walks. Two months later she was taking cabs to cooking school learning how to prepare the dishes. For a while she and I glowed with new-found health. I knew that her tumors still "held on for dear life," but that they were shrinking, passive, and no longer causing physical trauma.

And then, after a Thanksgiving holiday, where my first wife endured everyone else's festivities while she ate only vegetables, I returned home from work to find her chain-smoking cigarettes, saying that her fight days were over.

Janna died six months later of pneumonia, a year more then promised by her cancer doctors.

Thirty years later, with Laura, my second wife, I hold no desire to repeat the "delay" blunders of the past, and want to consider the diet/holistic tract from the get-go with a woman whom I consider perfect, both physically and psychologically.

With Laura, a black-belt karate trainer, I know that her mind/body strength can defeat cancer if we get her going on all fronts: toxin cleansing, nutrition optimization, immune system boosting, oxygen enhancement, energy balancing, on-going exercise, stress elimination, etc. ... and, hopefully, by performing innovative tactics that would really hurt cancer cells, referred to as *Infiltration*, my favorite part of the protocol.

I certainly do not want to submit to aggressive medical intervention that weakens Laura under the auspices of saving her. Laura possibly might accept the lumpectomy without cutting out the lymph nodes, but months of radiation grates against her survival instinct, and she makes that abundantly clear.

Instead, the day she learns of her diagnosis, Laura cuts out all sugars, white carbohydrates, wine, dairy, etc. Cancer cells need many times the amount of glucose sugar as do normal cells, so by going "cold turkey" sugar-wise, the patient cuts off the cancer's food supply that very day. Let's call it "zero tolerance."

Laura, "The Lioness" suddenly began the prowl!

But we stood only at the beginning of a comprehensive protocol to stymie the cancer.

I tell all of this to the crestfallen surgeon. And so, before scheduling a surgical procedure for the next week (as the surgeon had suggested at the top of the meeting), I say that we want to take a breath or two and think this through.

For one, we want to meet with a BRCA specialist to determine if Laura is genetically pre-disposed to Breast Cancer. The surgeon's office finds a BRCA analyst at the hospital for us to meet in a few days time, and we rescheduled to meet with the surgeon a second time a week later.

But upon breaking up the meeting, the surgeon cautions me, saying that Laura's 9 mm tumor holds over a billion cancer cells and the 4 mm tumor around 500 million. In addition, many cancer cells and micro-tumors likely lurk as well, too small to be detected.

These gigantic numbers get to us.

We leave feeling wobbly... and in trouble.

That night, I research the basics, to create ballast for our little boat, and I find answers for these questions:

What are the general medical issues of the breasts?

These are the breast conditions as cited on the American Medical Association (AMA) web site:

Fibroadenomas are fibrous, benign (noncancerous) growths in breast tissue. These growths are solid, usually painless lumps that are not attached to any structures in the breast. A fibroadenoma is usually removed surgically, using a local anesthetic.

A cyst is a fluid-filled sac. The cause of breast cysts is unknown. In the vast majority of cases, cysts are not harmful, although they may cause pain. Cysts disappear sometimes by themselves, or your doctor may draw out the fluid with a needle.

A breast abscess is a collection of pus, resulting from an infection. Symptoms may include tenderness and inflammation. Antibiotics are prescribed to treat the infection, and your doctor may drain the pus.

Fibrocystic breast disease is a common condition characterized by an increase in the fibrous and glandular tissues in the breasts, which results in small, nodular cysts, noncancerous lumpiness, and tenderness. Although called a "disease," this condition is not a disease. There is no specific treatment for fibrocystic disease (Note: I will suggest a treatment in chapter 18).

A tumor that is precancerous or cancerous usually shows up as a white area on a mammogram even before it can be felt. In cases where the tumor is cancerous, it may appear as a white area with radiating arms. A cancerous tumor may have no symptoms or may cause swelling, tenderness, discharge from the nipple or indentation of the nipple, or a dimpled appearance in the skin over the tumor. A breast biopsy is helpful in determining whether a mass is cancerous.

I also get a handle on the official stages of breast cancer, as follows:

. Stage 1A – Small tumors – less than 2 cm – growing in the original place the cancer developed (called "in situ").

. Stage 1B – Evidence that cancer cells have spread to the lymph nodes in the armpit.

. Stage 2A - The tumor has grown to 2-5 cm or three lymph nodes are infected.

. Stage 2B – The tumor has grown larger than 5 cm or four lymph nodes are infected.

. Stage 3 - Stage 3 breast cancer has extended beyond the immediate region of the tumor and may have invaded nearby lymph nodes and muscle.

. Stage 4 - Stage 4 breast cancer has spread to distant organs of the body.

Next I glean a basic understanding of the internal battlefield once cancer takes root, as follows:

How Does Cancer Spread? . Newly infected cells, now cancerous, are usually killed off by the immune system.

. Normal cells turning cancerous, becomes more common as one ages and as one's general health deteriorates.

. If the immune system falls behind, unchecked cancer cells form colonies (tumors).

. Tumors feed off of the body's blood system, capillaries at first, but then seek to envelope larger blood vessels to increase nutrients and their growth rate. With sustained nutrients, tumors can grow to many billions of cells in size.

After digesting all of the above until 5 am, I am ready to brief Laura, once awake, pretty pissed of that the doctors had not briefed us first.

Each night I pursed further research, attempting to connect all sorts of dots, my brain exhausted. I wanted to acquire an informed and measured position in advance of our next meeting with the breast surgeon, but this challenge proved daunting..

Chapter 2 - Getting Help

A week – seven days – is a lot of time in one sense, but no time whatsoever when you hold the dread of billions of cancer cells running loose.

As said, after first leaving the surgeon's office, I knew I would hop on the Internet and go into both cyber and book research mode six-to-10 hours per day, digging into the world of breast cancer to find protocols for each of the previously mentioned offensive fronts: diet, immune system, cleanses, etc.

But with heads swarming, Laura and I needed to meet with trusted advisors to fully sort things out prior to our next meeting with the surgeon. The first stop? Our local holistic doctor, and we met with her that very day right after the kick off-meeting with the surgeon. This holistic doctor treated many members of my family for nutritional supplementation, allergy identification, sprain healing (using photon – light - therapy), and to correct chiropractic conditions. I consider her an encyclopedia of alternative medicine.

From this meeting emerged three initiatives…

First, Laura would start a 14-day cleanse diet that included enzymes to relax her organs and fat cells into releasing deeply stored toxins and excess triglycerides.

Second, we would go to Boston to meet with a Thermography analyst who would identify points of trauma in Laura's body.

Third, the holistic doctor drew a blood sample and sent it to a lab to determine the level-of-absorption of 40 or so vitamins and minerals deep inside Laura's white blood cells. The findings from the lab would dictate the nutritional supplements needed.

The BRCA Meeting

Coming up next ahead of the Thermography trip to Boston, we make another trip to Hartford Hospital to meet with the BRCA specialist.

The American Cancer Society introduces BRCA as follows:

BRCA1 and BRCA2 are human genes that produce tumor suppressor proteins. These proteins help repair damaged DNA and, therefore, play a role in ensuring the stability of the cell's genetic material. When either of these genes is mutated, or altered, such that its protein product is not made or does not function correctly, DNA damage may not be repaired properly. As a result, cells are more likely to develop additional genetic alterations that can lead to cancer.

In other words, the BRAC genetic trait itself does not "cause" cancer. Instead it is a weakness – the inability to repair damaged DNA, whereby free radical and viral attacks on cells are allowed to succeed. I assume Angelina Jolie understood the distinction when electing for the double mastectomy.

We arrive expecting to have another blood test drawn and sent to the genetics lab for evaluation. Instead, Laura fills out a questionnaire about her family background, and the analyst enters these facts into a computer.

"Ta Da", the software package concludes that Laura's collective family and ethnic backgrounds make Laura <u>not</u> suitable for BRAC testing.

Apparently, we are neither getting a blood test nor even human expertise to weigh in on the matter at hand.

It takes me a while to decipher that a summary judgment was just delivered by a 28-year-old data input clerk. We figure that being in a life-and-death "cancer" situation, a definitive BRCA analysis report would be a good thing, and that a blood test would make perfect sense.

After mildly interrogating the analyst, I discover her to be an *Insurance Company Filter*. If your probability for BRAC is low, then "Insurance" is not required to cover the $5,000 tab for BRCA Testing!

The filter worked. The twenty-something clerk says that if we want to, we can pay the 5K ourselves, out-of-pocket. I said we would think about it… and we left.

That this Hartford Hospital service was a filter for the Insurance Companies was an eye opener. The silver lining to this mostly wasted day? The questionnaire told Laura that she possessed a low probability of BRCA deficiency. But as you might guess, I hate probability statistics when we can obtain clear data.

I would reconsider BRCA testing down the road once we lined up the other ducks.

BTW, we paid for this ridiculous meeting with our credit card, out-of pocket.

The Thermography Meeting

Two days later we witnessed the clever world of Thermography in action. The basis of this test holds that traumatized areas of the body retain concentrations of warm blood, as blood delivers Platelets, T-cells, Killer Cells, and Stem Cells to the area in trouble.

We can identify these areas of blood concentration by placing the body as a whole in a cold surrounding, where blood, in general, rushes to the body's core to protect the organs, with only the traumatized spots left still holding significant levels of warm blood. Normal areas become cool, but traumatized areas remain warm.

It was a two-and-one-half-hour drive from Connecticut to the outskirts of Boston, but we eventually found the building.

The waiting room held books on diet, et. al., that I perused. I remained skeptical about what would come next, even though I understood the straightforward premise of the whole Thermography program.

The analyst proved a veteran in her field of expertise, competent and articulate. She first measured 100 body surface temperature points on Laura's head, neck, and torso in a comfortable temperature setting.

Once these readings registered, she cooled the room, and activated fans, thus causing body chills. The analyst re-measured the 100 temperature points, and thus identified three points of trauma:

In the jaw, at tooth numbers 3 and 4
In the valve between the small and large intestine
In the thyroid gland

With these findings, things grew very interesting…

First, Laura's only lifetime dental issues comprised an extracted tooth #3, eight years prior, and a root canal on tooth #4 one-year prior.

Second, a Kinesiologist (one who measures energy flow blockages in the body) had recently identified a weakness in Laura's small/large colon valve area (she complained of bloating/pain) and had given Laura exercises to strengthen the area. These exercises greatly improved her condition, yet some sensation remained.

Third, Laura's thyroid condition had been treated with T3/T4 supplements for around six years as her thyroid gland was apparently failing to deliver these needed hormones.

More compelling was that the Energy Meridian (the Life Force channel) that went through the cancerous tumors on Laura's right breast, started at the traumatized tooth numbers 3 and 4, and ran to the traumatized intestinal valve – point-to-point. An immediate possibility was that the level of life force energy flowing down the meridian through the infected breast area was chaotic, preventing breast cells and local immune cells from getting the energy reinforcement (stimulus) needed to fight off disease.

Besides these findings, the Thermography Analyst gave me the name of a cancer clinic in Mexico that she urged us to consider.

Back home the next day, we report the events to our Holistic Doctor and, based upon the findings, she next recommends a Biological Dentist who can weigh in on the role of the traumatized teeth.

We make an appointment to meet this doctor and make a reciprocal appointment with a Gastroenterologist to get a colonoscopy performed on Laura, to examine her colon's connecting valve with the small intestine.

We made these appointments two weeks out, so for now, Laura did the 14-day cleanse our Holistic Doctor recommended, and we put the Kinesiologist, whom we had initially consulted for abdomen pain, in charge of balancing Laura's overall energy levels, using Chiropractic and Acupuncture means on a weekly basis.

I looked into the Mexican clinic.

<u>Mexico</u>

I find the Mexican Doctor's *Hope4Cancer* website. It offers a heavy-duty, on-site, three-week assault on cancer, including the full-cancer diet, body heating (as cancer hates elevated body temperatures), IV injections (such as vitamin C), and the centerpiece: *Photon/Sonic Oxygen Activation Therapy.*

The patient ingests a compound that only the cancer cells absorb. When subjected to certain light and sound frequencies, this compound chemically unravels, releasing huge amounts of oxygen (cancer hates oxygen) into the cancerous tumor.

To trigger the oxygen release, the patient lies in a chamber (not unlike a tanning chamber), which directs light and sound waves into the body, breaking down the ingested compound inside the cancer cells and releasing oxygen to sicken and kill the cancer.

It sounded like the perfect *infiltration* strategy.

I searched many WEB sites of prominent research hospitals in America, and found that a number of institutions in the United States had, in fact, experimented with *Photon/Sonic Oxygen Activation.*

It apparently works, yet, for some reason, has not entered the mainstream. From what I read,, the Mexican doctor, gets credit for refining the compound to the point where it only affects the cancer cells.

It took a week, but I finally got to speak to the Mexican doctor, who I found to be very grounded, worldly, and a capable fellow on all accounts. But ultimately Laura and I passed on his approach (for now), as it weighed heavy in application and long in distance, calling for us to be away for almost a month.

Laura appeared in good health, and so I first wanted to see what we could do locally, remaining centered at home with our four children.

Had Laura been a Stage 3-4 case, we may have committed to the three-week program to kick-start the recovery (the Mexico program continues once one returns home with some of the approaches described in this book).

I would first have wanted more insight into the clinics results. Certainly, some people have had success there, but is it 1 in 10, 1 in 100, and for what caners –tumor or blood?

The Second Meeting with the Surgeon

Our seven days passed and we went back into Hartford to reconvene with the breast surgeon. He appeared to understand our research and motivation, and said he did not dismiss any of it, even the Chinese Meridians, etc.

But one had to wonder, he postured, if we wanted to live like this, eating limited foods and tending to an elaborate self-help program that held no scientific basis.

Or we could simply do a lumpectomy and get on with life.

We agreed the holistic diet/cleanse approach held no real science, just common sense, but I asserted the surgical approach held no science either, for it merely comprised a body of statistics. True science, I pointed out, explores root causes and effects, not merely probabilities.

I explained our deep-seated fear that in the absence of science, medical intervention pursued neither a root cause nor lasting cure, so we would always be looking over our shoulders.

Alternatively, if we could concoct an organic process of reducing tumor size – proving the body could control the disease – then yes, a lumpectomy (a one-hour procedure) might be warranted, but we could then skip the dreaded six-week radiation follow-up phase.

Instead, we would continue with the then-proven holistic measures to kill off the unseen cells left behind after popping out the visible tumors.

Intriguing, yes, the surgeon agreed, but he first wanted us to meet with a radiologist who would make a strong case to do the radiation anyway.

His nurse sets up the radiologist meeting, and the surgeon has us sign a document so that another meeting is not be needed, just a phone call to schedule a surgery time slot. He *had* proved patient.

Later on I realized that at no point did anyone ever mention the cost of a lumpectomy plus 50 days of radiation. The cancer world – with 10 million insured American patients paying in unmentionable amounts of money, year-upon-year - certainly makes for a strange "cottage industry"...

The Radiologist Visit

A few days later, the radiation doctor spells out much of the same statistical stuff as had the surgeon. My optic focuses upon gauging the danger of *not* doing the radiation, and with this as my focus, a number of interesting points surface.

First, the doctor estimates that the big tumor has been growing for years, maybe as long as eight-to-10 years (which, by the way, corresponded to the infection and extraction of Laura's #3 tooth, and her thyroid issues).

Upon her saying this, I wonder about all of the undetectable cancer missed by mammograms and MRIs. I pose that chemotherapy (not her line of treatment) might be a better "mopping up" tactic as it would hit every cancer cell anywhere in the body.

The doctor dismisses this, stating that radiation of the right breast and armpit has better statistical outcomes in these Stage 1 circumstances. I point out that this is only valid in the five-year time horizon. She responds that longer dated statistics are not available, so that radiation appears the clearest choice.

The paradox does not dawn on the highly educated doctor, who also must have posted some serious SAT and MetCat scores in her day.

She just said that the cancer was probably in development for a decade, yet her statistics on success are tied to merely five years. Yes, with radiation, one could have a good five-year result with just the right breast, as other developing cancers elsewhere in the body would only surface later. I ignore this cockeyed presentation without saying a word.

Finally I ask if the radiation devices now in use are the same as those employed 30 years back and she replies, "Basically, yes."

Still, I take away an important framework: if it took Laura's tumor that long to get its footing, then we could go weeks, even months attempting to blunt the tumor's progress before crying "uncle" and signing up for surgery/radiation.

We could get a series of sonograms, say, every six weeks, and decide what to do at each checkpoint.

With this insight, I, the bold non-victim, feel the weight of fear quickly receding. Laura, the actual cancer patient, does not feel so confident or clear.

Under the circumstances, fear dominates her psyche at every point, and understandably so. A lumpectomy with radiation would silence the fear, at least for a few years. The temporary silencing of fear proves the biggest motivator in saying "yes" to standard medical intervention.

As the days go by, we talk about this many times, and with so many people saying we should effectively "stop screwing around," the passive surgery/radiation path appears pretty good at many a midnight hour.

The Colonoscopy

When Colonoscopy day comes up, Laura says that the ill feelings in her gut have already disappeared after eight weeks of doing the "gut" exercises assigned by the Kenisiologist. We go ahead with the exam regardless, just to be sure.

I admire this Gastronomic doctor and his diligence. And so, we are pleased to hear of no visible problems with the large or small intestines or with the connecting valve.

While chatting in the recovery room with the doctor about the good findings, I mention the Meridian Path observations stumbled upon regarding intestine valve discomfort and traumatized teeth. He dismisses it all as "nonsense."

Ok, so he doesn't subscribe to the "find the root cause" approach. Still, his "all clear" report means we are narrowing down the moving parts.

A Laser Treatment Option Surfaces

As said, each night I did research on the Internet. One night I investigated experimental protocols for cancer taking place across the United States.

At Columbia-Presbyterian Hospital in Manhattan – near enough to my Connecticut residence no less – I find what appears a perfect solution: a facility using a heat laser to directly kill tumor cells, with only the incision of a hollow needle affecting the breast.

The protocol: through the needle's hollow chamber, a heat laser beam flows that immediately kills any cells it encounters. One uses a sonogram guide to target the tumor, bit-by-bit.

That morning I phone the doctor's office at Columbia-Presbyterian and make an appointment for a few weeks out.

In the meantime, I arrange to send all of Laura's MRI, ultrasound, and mammogram "films" to Columbia-Presbyterian, and have Hartford Hospital's Pathology Lab mail the biopsy specimen.

We hold great expectations, as a laser expedites the killing of visible cancer tumors to an hour's time, and one could still consider mopping up any hidden cancer cells and/or colonies via the diet/cleanse approach, rather than through radiation/chemotherapy.

Candidly, at the time, we lacked confidence that we could kill the tumors on our own. And so, zapping them with a laser beam looked pretty good. I just couldn't figure out why more professionals do not apply this approach to *all* visible tumor-based cancer cases.

As our appointment stood two weeks away, "getting more info" about this option would have to wait. But first, our meeting with the Biological Dentist approached, so next I turned my nighttime research sessions toward understanding the "exotic" *Biological Dentistry* topic, but, more so, to understand cancer itself... the world of *cells*, *toxins*, and the *viruses* that infect weakened cells.

Chapter 3 – The War On Cancer

"Back at the ranch," I pursue my internet research, usually working until 3 am each night, sometimes ordering related books on Amazon, and reading them cover-to-cover as well. Because I studied cancer in my previous life back in the 70s and 80s during my first wife's episode, I held a certain curiosity as to what might've changed in the medical world.

Not much, it seemed.

The Chemo had grown more "targeted," i.e., more devastating to the specific cancer cell type, although this approach still poisoned every cell in the body in the attempt to attack this one cell type, and, still, no one discussed root causes.

The American Cancer Society's main website page still claims that they do not know what causes cancer, skirting the issue by saying it comprises a collection of "factors." They only refer to known risk factors, such as cigarette smoking, never saying what exactly happens when a good lung cell suddenly turns cancerous.

After 50 years or so of "The War On Cancer," for the medical community to still not offer a definitive cause-and-effect framework seems astonishing.

No wonder the whole medical world focuses on cancer *removal* options using the same-old, same-olds: incredibly expensive surgery, poisonous chemotherapy, and debilitating radiation "treatments," rather than nipping cancer in the bud by isolating and removing its germinating enablers at the cellular level.

Chemotherapy

Let's look at door number three, chemotherapy.

Chemotherapy – meaning, "curing with drugs" – got its start from experiments with mustard gas stockpiles leftover from World War I. Researchers turned the mustard agent (breathed as a burning gas) into a poison that could be infused into the bloodstream.

The idea started (and remains) to take advantage of cancer's very active metabolism and rapid cell division rates to absorb poison more aggressively than other cells.

And this is indeed how chemotherapy works; every cell is poisoned to some degree, with the cancer cells getting it the worst.

The poison, though, seriously harms any normal cell that also has fairly high metabolism and cell division rates. These "up-tempo" cells include hair cells, bone marrow cells, stomach, and intestine cells.

The punishment these innocent cells endure during chemotherapy results in the familiar effects: hair loss, lowered blood counts, nausea, fatigue, and infections. Not only does chemotherapy weaken all cells, but also the chemo drug itself is acidic, causing an overall septic condition to settle in throughout the body.

The net result: permanent weakening of the bone marrow, reduced ability to absorb essential nutrients, and emboldened tumors that grow resistant to "chemo" poison ... all with nothing accomplished to prevent another bout of cancer to incubate at a future date.

With so much negativity surrounding chemotherapy, you might expect a societal pushback of sorts, with chemotherapy seen as the modern-day version of bloodletting.

Instead, the chemotherapy religion remains stronger than ever.

Consider the following taking place in my home state...

On January 3, 2015, Connecticut's newspaper of record, the *Hartford Courant*, reported a story of a 17-year-old girl forced by the State Department of Children and Families to accept Chemotherapy against her will ("...for her own good..." they claimed). She suffered from Hodgkins Lymphoma, the same cancer from which my first wife suffered. The article explained that the chemo "worked", justifying the whole Orwellian directive.

One final note on chemotherapy: Post-Chemotherapy Cognitive Impairment (aka Chemo Brain) is a condition resulting in changes in memory, and fluency, affecting many patients treated aggressively with chemo drugs.

What are the top six cancer incidents in America?

#1 Breast Cancer – with 235,000 new cases per year

#2 Prostate Cancer – 233,000 new cases per year

#3 Lung Cancer – 224,000 new cases per year

#4 Colon Cancer – 96,000 new cases per year

#5 Skin Cancer – 81,000 new cases per year

#6 Brain Cancer – 23,000 new cases per year

That's 800,000 new top category cancer cases per year in the U.S. alone, with none of the many rare cases counted. And, most telling, the death rate per 1,000 due to cancer in America has remained stagnant for decades.

The survival rate to five years remains the only improvement. If you are willing to endure surgery, poisoning, and radiation, you might delay death for a short while. And before signing up for treatment, your statistical survival chances are spelled out, making the service offering above board and therefore an ethical proposition.

But many things are not pointed out: not a whisper about Post-Chemotherapy Cognitive Impairment (aka Chemo Brain), for instance, the steady death rate from cancer over the decades, or the possibilities of self-healing as an alternative.

So much for our "War on Cancer."

PART II

UNDERSTANDING CANCER

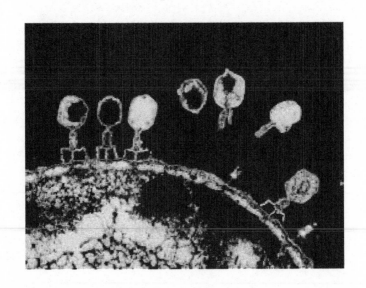

Viruses attacking a cell

Chapter 4 – Understanding Cells

It's About the Cells, the Repository of Life

Something turns normal cells cancerous, and Chapter 6 will lay out the *virus* theory I support. Here in Chapter 4, I will outline the structure of cellular life as the foundation of more to come. Let's start off with the big picture on life itself – the fundamentals – and then look deeper into cells.

What Is Life? *It is multi-dimensional…*

Our <u>Biological Dimension</u> – Human life in its smallest form exists as a cell. Each cell is a *Biochemical Factory* filled with *Molecular/Electrical Activity*. The cell's DNA/RNA – a vast library of *Chemical Formula Templates* accumulated by each species over generations – directs the molecular activities. An electrically charged *Life Energy Grid* pulsating through the body "commands" cells to operate according to their DNA/RNA chemical formulas. When this *Life Energy* driver "disappears" at death, the cellular biochemical processes halt and we proclaim the entire body "dead" – full stop!

Our <u>Mental Dimension</u> – Whereas one's DNA/RNA library holds *Inherited Biochemical Knowledge* that directs and protects the cell, one's mental dimension deals with the here and now, directing the body via the nervous system, *somehow* storing *Sensory-gleaned Experiential Knowledge* within the neurons of the brain.

Collectively, the brain, a *Mental Control System,* starts with instinct and further builds a database of acquired knowledge. Some believe that the mind can do even more, claiming that one's state-of-mind can cause – and cure – disease.

Our Consciousness Dimension – Consciousness comprises something more than organized *Biochemical Factories* powered by a *Life Energy Grid* coordinated by a *Mental Control System* – for example, Zebras possess all of this.

Consciousness, which, on Earth I believe only humans possess, exists where one holds awareness of one's own thinking. Consciousness exists in addition to the biological and mental life dimensions, and probably bridges a spiritual world of ideas to ourselves. Knowledge, deciphered and categorized via consciousness, can possibly survive death and find its way back to the spirit side.

The limited focus of this book claims that our consciousness allows us to envision cures and organize them into effective protocols. Consciousness fosters wisdom, hence we are called "sapiens," the Latin for "wisdom," as in *Homo Sapiens.*

The World Of Cells

Cells make up the basis of all living things… from bacteria to plants to animals. Each cell devours oxygen and nutrients to fuel its biochemical requirements according to the needs set forth by that cell's DNA playbook.

The DNA issues orders to the rest of the cell by releasing RNA chemical templates that tell the cell what to do. The released RNA triggers millions of chemical reactions inside and outside of the cell's wall.

These combined DNA/RNA templates are inherited, refined over countless generations toward protecting cells from disease and for governing each cell's "proper" behavior.

Moreover, the DNA/RNA templates of each tiny cell work collectively with the other cells of our bodies, not unlike a trillion-member symphony orchestra, wherein each orchestra member fits in with ensemble "exactitude," knowing its "part to play."

Referring to cells as "biological factories" hardly constitutes an exaggeration. Each cell possesses compartments allowing for specialization inside of the cell, e.g., the nucleus compartment (the "executive suite"), the mitochondria compartment (the "power station"), and the peroxisome compartment (the "chemistry lab"), etc.

Inside the cell, molecular exchanges called "proton pumps" send enormous amounts of electrical charges around to keep everything running. The cell runs similar to a factory, yet *alive*, able to get sick, able to heal itself, able to divide, and able to die.

There are simple cell beings and complex cell beings. Bacteria, for example, exist as simple cell beings.

In multi-celled human beings, cells must specialize in their purpose to support this more-complex living structure, comprising skin, blood, bone, etc.

Humans possess more than 100 specialized cells (and, by the way, around the same number of cancer types).

Estimates put humans housing more than 100 trillion cells, all pumping away inside of us in super-real time (I'll use 100 trillion cells as a reference point)

Cell Division "Mitosis" & Programmed Cell Death "Apoptosis"

In addition to the DNA/RNA guided chemistry, which takes place inside the cell, a world of communicative chemistry takes place outside of the cell, where the cell communicates with the body via further molecular signals.

Certain chemical commands (steroids) direct cells to either divide (mitosis) or die (apoptosis) — from the Greek.

Healthy cells will divide or die on command by the body's signals; conversely, cancer cells will ignore the die signals, exactly as viruses do (more on this at book's end).

The balance between dividing cells and dying cells carries paramount importance. If cells only divide and never die, the body would grow indefinitely. Likewise, the command for cells to die must not "go overboard" if cell populations are to sustain the body in specific locations.

For example, as one ages, due to factors such as vitamin, mineral, protein, and hormone deficiencies, muscle cells die faster than the creation of their replacements, and the body experiences a slow pattern of muscle loss.

Bone weakening provides another common example of the aging factor, though in addition to an imbalance in new/old cells, bone weakening also includes changes to the bone-cell calcium and phosphate content. Age unravels more than one thing. In complex beings, cells die after a set period of time – skin cells, within weeks; blood cells, in 60 days, and bone cells, years.

The rate of cell division must keep pace with this timeline of programmed cell death. Uncertainty exists as to which cells will die, although the body apparently chooses "sick" cells quickly due to molecular signals distressed cells emit (more on cellular "SOS's" later).

The test called "Serum TK," described in the *Living Wisely* chapter, measures the body's overall relationship between dividing and dying cells. High levels of Serum TK in adults indicate cancerous activity (runaway division), even if mammograms and other tests cannot "see" the cancer.

Cell division during childhood/menstrual cycles

Early on, as the body grows during infancy and childhood, most specialized cells divide more rapidly than die (experienced as "growth spurts") until the human reaches adulthood.

Once maturity arrives, the body somehow maintains the balance between cell division and cell death, similar perhaps to a self-balancing gyroscope.

Only a few parts of the body still engage in cell divisions that exceed the rate of dying cells. An important example of this – *for the purposes of this book* – comprises the cells of the breast and uterus.

Each month, the body releases quantities of estrogen, a hormone/steroid that instructs female sex cells to multiply rapidly in anticipation of the woman becoming pregnant. If pregnancy does not happen, the body purges the new cells via menstruation (More on estrogen and menstrual scaring later).

Trauma and stem cells

When trauma occurs — when cells suffer damage, e.g., in an ankle sprain – then the troubled domain broadcasts an alert to attract platelets, T-cells, and stem cells, which rush to the site of the embattled cells to arrest trauma and begin the healing process.

But the resolution of trauma takes time. As a reference point, stem cells take up to 60 days to replace a bag of blood donated to the Red Cross, and up to 120 days to shore-up damaged muscle.

Again, these repair activities are not achieved via specialized cells themselves dividing and dying in their normal rhythm, but through replacement stem cells moving in. Stem cells "born" with neutral chromosome settings, mature into specialized cells by copying the settings of the cell they are replacing. (Chromosome switch settings that craft specific cellular types, are described later).

Cells Not Programmed to Die

Only three types of human cells are not programmed to die: stem cells, heart muscle cells, and neuron cells in the brain.

Stem cells residing in the bone marrow do not live and then die inside the marrow. Instead, stem cells prolifically divide to keep trillions on hand for dispersal by the billions each day into the blood stream to serve as either specialized replacement cells (for injured body parts) or as new blood cells.

However, each time cells divide – bone marrow cells, skin cells, retina cells, hair cells – they lose a bit of genetic data, much as audio quality deteriorates when copying a recording from tape… to tape… to tape.

As we age to the point where the cell pool has already divided, i.e., been copied, hundreds of times, a meaningful amount of genetic precision erosion results. Thus, weaker body-part cells enter play over time.

Deterioration of genetic data offers one major reason that age so significantly affects our general level of health, and inherently moves us closer to the tipping points of cancer and to natural death.

Our cells simply do not know what to do, and become vulnerable to outside elements like toxins, viruses, funguses, bacteria and parasites. On the other hand, the 20 billion brain neurons that mature by the age of 26 – when our frontal lobe stops growing "white matter" – are the only ones we get. No stem cell services create new neurons. Neurons simply fade away as we age, losing one percent over a lifetime.

One of the reasons that Dementia surfaces in our later years, is likely due to rogue proteins that corrode brain and nerve cells, not to loss of cells.

Because neuron cells do not divide, their original genetic precision stays intact, and so as long as they are not debased by bad proteins, they prove increasingly effective.

A good protein called Brain-derived Neurotrophic Factor (a growth hormone) helps to repair and grow nerves, and create new synapse links amongst the neurons, but it is unclear if this protein can lead to new neurons being generated to replace dying or damaged neuron cells.

Likewise, heart muscle cells sit fixed for life. We have the same amount of heart cells when born as when we die. They simply expand as we grow. When "heart attacks" damage one's heart, it remains damaged for life. I pondered that neither neurons nor heart cells divide; yet brain cancer occurs but not heart cancer. I wrote to the American Cancer Society about this; they acknowledged my email, but never responded. Later I found an article explaining that "binder" grey and white matter cells that do divide surround brain neurons, and these binder cells become cancerous, sometimes via infection, and sometimes via metastasis from other infected areas of the body.

Chapter 5 – Understanding Toxins

Toxins Cause Acidity and Free Radical Formation

Next we look at the things beyond age that weaken cells, thus creating a vulnerability to cancer.

Four subjects linked to cancer include "Toxins, Acidity, Free Radicals, and Anti-Oxidants," but they really constitute a single, interrelated phenomenon.

It all starts with toxins, which include environmental and ingested chemicals, plus natural and man-made radiation. These foreign elements transform one's healthy biochemistry into a destabilized, inflamed and polluted environment, where bodily fluids become pro-cancer "acidic," and renegade molecules called "free radicals" corrode healthy cells. Ugh!

Toxins form the common denominator to the entire paradigm, and any attempt to fight cancer that does not include a complete scrubbing of toxins from the body conjures the effectiveness of washing dishes in dirty water.

Comprehending the vastness of one's body chemistry proves a daunting task. Trillions of coordinated, life-sustaining, chemical combinations take place each second in and around the cells, all without causing unwanted molecular bi-products that harm the cells.

To achieve this level of absolute perfection and balance, body chemistry remains a closed, self-contained, perpetually balanced system, except for one small problem: *outside chemicals and radiation (the toxins) penetrate the body!* One ingests, inhales, or absorbs these foreign substances from the outside, and they trigger a slew of unwanted chemical exchanges resulting in the mentioned "acidity" and "free radical" outcomes.

Let's look at acidity first.

Acidity, Aerobic, and Anaerobic Energy Creation

The body comprises 70 percent salt water, basically the same as the salt concentration as ocean water, both very *alkaline* and able to hold oxygen.

Acidity, in contrast to alkalinity, *squeezes out* oxygen. And so, over the years, as one accumulates acidic chemicals into one's cells, oxygen levels decline; the normal cells experience a type of suffocation, and developing cancer cells – which do not use oxygen to generate energy – enjoy an acidic "field day" all to themselves.

Ninety-nine percent of the time normal cells use oxygen to burn nutrients (*called aerobic metabolism*) – like burning firewood. Cancer cells (similar to viruses) do not burn with oxygen, and instead rely upon chemical fermentation (blending chemicals together, like a whisky still) to create energy for themselves (*called anaerobic metabolism*).

While all cells possess the potential for both aerobic and anaerobic methods, the body remains primarily oxygen-based and only uses the anaerobic chemical fermentation method when pushed.

Hence, acidic build-up, after years of accumulating toxins in one's system, becomes a dangerous state into which to succumb, as it nudges the body away from oxygen methods towards anaerobic reliance. And to make matters worse, no clues indicate this danger.

An interesting way of understanding aerobic/anaerobic processes follows: long distant runners use both, as the oxygen method alone would not generate sufficient energy to sustain their efforts. The runners' muscle cells, besides devouring oxygen, use painful anaerobic methods to tap directly into the body's glucose reserves to provide more stamina via chemical mixing (hence the common practice of devouring carbohydrates prior to a race).

Once the race concludes, the body returns to aerobic methods. A by-product of the racer's anaerobic experience? The creation of lactic acid, which further acidifies the body.

Free Radicals

Environmental and ingested toxic chemicals causing acidity also interact with other chemicals in the body triggering "free radicals".

Free radicals occur when toxins come in contact with living tissue, whereby atomic-level protons and electrons mix and match into new molecular combinations.

In this "Wild West" chemical setting, "free radicals" form when a molecule's proton and electron counts do not equal one another.

A free radical remains standing as a leftover, the molecule stuck without a chair in "Musical Molecules," missing a proton or electron, when the chemical music stops.

To correct this proton/electron imbalance, the "radicalized" molecule "robs" elements from nearby healthy cells, creating instability in their molecules.

These, in turn, steal what they need from the next molecule in the cellular neighborhood... and so on, causing a vast chain-reaction in and outside of the cells, as electrons and protons are wrested away from stable molecules to make other molecules whole. The chain reaction progresses like a prairie fire, reaching the cell's "proud" DNA, itself "shockingly" robbed of its electrons and protons, thereby damaging DNA "instruction" genes and gene switch settings, leaving the cell unable to operate or divide correctly.

This perversion of DNA either leads directly to a cancerous cell division via "spontaneous" mutation (one theory), or it so weakens the cell that viruses can penetrate the DNA and take over via switch settings (proposed in this book).

Either way, cancer can result.

A question: The ability of molecules to carry unbalanced electrical charges is called ionization. What I have not been able to determine is why some forms of ionization are damaging, with others beneficial. Free radicals, for example, are harmful, eating away at the cells. Electrolytes (described later) are charged molecules essential for keeping adequate electron supplies within the cells and cause no damage. Hmm.

More On Anaerobic (Non-Oxygen) Metabolism

A key insight on how the chain reaction onslaught of free radicals leads to cancer is the effect of free radicals on the tiny mitochondria (the cell's energy producers, described in detail in the *Boosting Energy* chapter).

Basically, each cell relies upon mitochondria (bacteria-like microbes *living* inside each cell) to create energy for that cell. The mitochondria take in nutrients and "burn" the nutrients with incoming supplies of oxygen. If the little buggers suffer damage, or if the cell becomes very destabilized by high acidity or free radical chain reactions, the mitochondria die.

When this happens the cell's whole power station crew shuts down, and the cell remains left to its own devices to survive. The cell achieves survival by switching over to *anaerobic metabolism*, the back-up method (the long-distance runner's auxiliary method), not using oxygen.

Instead of burning oxygen, the cell ferments chemical combinations that give off heat and electrical charges to create a replacement source of energy.

Anaerobic metabolism processes draw heavily on sugars present in the blood stream as the main ingredient of their chemical mixing concoction. Cancer cells use this same sugar-based formula to generate energy, foregoing oxygen, and instead metabolizing sugars, the lifeline of cancer.

And so, though a cell damaged by free radicals may not possess all of the attributes of cancer, such as multiplying freely and metastasizing into new cell forms, etc., the damaged cell contains one key cancerous feature already in operation: *routine anaerobic digestion.*

A full-blown cancer only needs a virus to penetrate its DNA, to propel aberrant RNA orders into the cell, probably `via simple switch settings, not via mass DNA mutations.

Radiation

Radiation and cancer correlate very closely. The probability of cancer increases with the radiation dose one receives, and so, theories exist that radiation itself causes DNA mutations turning a normal cell cancerous.

This assumes that radiation's cell-damaging method, also a form of "ionization," (the creation of electron mismatches), can perfectly mutate an entire set of chromosomes and switch settings, to work in perfect concert with each other, behaving as a fundamentally new type of cell.

This constitutes an unimaginable set of coincidences aligning. Instead, like all other carcinogens, radiation ionization causes free radicals to directly reach down to the DNA level (called chromosome "breaks"). This makes radiation just one more way of weakening cells, exposing damaged cells to a viral takeover that infuses viral "DNA switch" agendas.

Life exposes us to cosmic radiation (from the universe) at all times, but we add to this unavoidable fixed dosage every time we subject ourselves to an X-ray or mammogram.

If you also get radiation treatment to kill cancer, then big dosage numbers come into play, which can encourage further outbreaks of cancer down the line.

As stated earlier, I can imagine circumstances where radiation would offer a reasonable choice to supplement a cancer protocol, but it remains a trade-off of survival horizon bets that radiation doctors never discuss.

Oxidative Stress and Anti-oxidants

Oxygen constitutes one of the important paradoxes of life on Earth in its dual role as both friend and foe. We all understand the "friend" part every time we hold our breath... and crave oxygen. The "foe" part of the relationship appears less apparent; the ability of oxygen to burn things ...and not just logs on the fire.

Oxygen burns living matter (cells), if an oxygen-proof skin does not protect the cells.

For example, an apple's skin protects the apple from the air, but once cut open, the internal apple cells become oxidized; they turn brown and quickly putrefy.

With humans, our skin is oxygen proof, as is the lung tissue that transports oxygen to the oxygen-proof red blood cells. But like an apple, our internal cells remain vulnerable to "oxidization" (by incoming oxygen). Thankfully, anti-oxidants come to the rescue.

Anti-oxidants provide a protective covering that encapsulates each cell's outer membrane, a "chemical skin" of sorts.

This covering shields the general membrane from the incoming oxygen, allowing specialized membrane receptors to absorb oxygen in an orderly manner and direct oxygen to its proper destination inside of the cell.

Simply speaking, a cell membrane receptor is a molecule sitting on the cell wall that presents a certain puzzle shape to which an outside molecule with a reciprocal shape can bind. All biochemical activities revolve around endless sets of receptor molecules seeking to bind with each other. The ENOX receptor controlling cell death/division will be discussed in detail at the end of the book.

Anti-oxidant protective molecules comprise vitamins, such as vitamins A, C and E, and are provisioned by the food we eat.

Some foods, such as *blueberries*, contain much higher concentrations of anti-oxidant support than other foods – hot dogs come to mind as a poor antioxidant. Good anti-oxidant supplements exist, as well. I will discuss the antioxidant food and supplement sources in the *Diet Supplements* chapter.

But should one not have an adequate supply of anti-oxidants on hand, oxygen will find exposed membranes and oxidize the molecules it encounters.

This destructive chemical process, in turn, creates "offspring" free radicals, so now the cell is being burnt while also being chemically destabilized by the chain reactions caused by the free radicals. When we speak about ways to weaken cells, to make them vulnerable to virus and ultimately to cancer, oxidative stress is on top of the list.

An interesting observation follows: Lemons are a great anti-oxidant food source. Many chefs squeeze lemon juice over cut fruit to keep it from turning brown. Yet fresh squeezed lemon juice is a great cancer fighting food for a second reason as well. It is counterintuitive, but citric lemon juice also causes an alkaline response in the body, as chemically, the juice reduces the need for stomach acid generation.

Triggers in the stomach encountering lemon acid, sense that enough acid is in play, and do not call upon the stomach glands to produce even more. Reduced stomach acid means that high acidity does not reach the intestines for absorption into the bloodstream. Lemons are very good for you, and the famous "Mediterranean Diet" has plenty of lemon in it.

Here's the kicker: As bad as free radicals are, overall, they also serve a purpose. Immune system cells use both oxygen and free radicals as weapons to attack viruses and bacteria lurking in the body. We need certain free radicals, just not every kind, and not too many of those that come in handy.

The obvious goal remains to keep the right balance between free radicals and anti-oxidants, and this requires three steps:

1. Detoxify the body of outside chemicals that have built up inside of the cells (described in How to Detoxify), and

2. Consume enough anti-oxidant foods together with anti-oxidant supplements to shield against oxidative stress (described in the Diet chapter).

3. Stay clear of radiation (a self-evident proposition).

Speaking of radiation, here is a quote from Doctor Blaylot, who publishes health advisories.

An area of medicine that is badly neglected is protecting patients from radiation damage caused by radiological procedures, including CT scans, PET scans, X-rays, mammograms, and injection of radioactive dyes.

The danger goes beyond the period of exposure. Damage done by radiation is cumulative and long lasting — which means that each X-ray does more damage, and it builds up over time.

When I was practicing neurosurgery, doctors were told by radiologists that CT scans exposed patients to very little radiation. But now we know that a single CT scan can contain radiation that's equal to hundreds of chest X-rays.

But before looking at ways to detoxify yourself, or to use diet to stabilize your system, we'll next look at how viruses take advantage of polluted and depleted systems; the cause of cancer.

Chapter 6 – Understanding Viruses

The Seeds of Cancer

We have looked at cells and the toxic factors that weaken cells, so now let's get a feel for the trillions of viruses lying in wait inside and outside of our bodies, searching for vulnerable cells off which to live.

The language below elaborates the "virus" theory, mentioned earlier, one that I adhere to regarding cancer's root cause, acknowledging that no "science" *per se* exists to fully back this theory up.

Instead the "viral" explanation simply makes sense, the way Charles Darwin's "natural selection" theory makes sense in describing *variation within a species* (as this, too, still has no "science" to prove it).

And lest you think I am hanging out on a limb by myself, I found the following statement buried inside The American Cancer Society's Web Site, listed under "Viruses", but not under "Cancers":

Viruses are very small organisms; most can't even be seen with an ordinary microscope. They are made up of a small group of genes in the form of DNA or RNA surrounded by a protein coating.

Viruses need to enter a living cell and "hijack" the cell's machinery to reproduce and make more viruses. Some viruses do this by inserting their own DNA (or RNA) into that of the host cell. When the DNA or RNA affects the host cell's genes, it may push the cell toward becoming cancer.

Who knows, the American Cancer Society probably has different camps inside of its own walls, each vying for different theories, each neutralizing the other's ability to proclaim their views to the outside world.

So we are on our own. I am on my own!

The World of Viruses

In addition to the vast world of cellular beings, the world of viruses exists: extremely small entities, bigger than atoms, but more than 1/1000 smaller than a cell.

Viruses, so stripped down in what they can do, cannot live on their own, and therefore must invade and live off of cells in parasite fashion.

Virus entities are not pre-programmed to die, and do not die until destroyed.

For example, chicken pox viruses live inside of humans for decades and often surface later in life in the form of "shingles." Outside of living bodies, viruses can lie dormant for decades, in dust and other inert substances, brought back to *activity (not life)* when making contact with glucose inside a living being.

Some biologists say that viruses are not true living beings, but are instead highly complex chemical systems that become "active" when chemically stimulated by cellular glucose. When a virus penetrates a cell, viral DNA starts to release RNA chemical commands to the cell, making the cell do the bidding of the virus. Tactically, viral DNA becomes a re-programming force, recalling "HAL," the spaceship's computer in the movie "2001: A Space Odyssey," that executes a "takeover" game plan against the cell it has infiltrated.

For an amazing look at viruses in action, check out a vivid animation documentary on the virus/cell battle ground, produced in England, at the URL:

http://www.dailymotion.com/video/x1f26gz_bbc-our-secret-universe-the-hidden-life-of-the-cell-720p-hdtv_tech

View it yourself and be amazed!

Viruses hate oxygen; oxygen is poison to them. Unlike cells, which oxidize nutrients (burning nutrients like logs on a fire, drafting vast flows of oxygen from the bloodstream), viruses get "free" energy from the host's glucose, allowing the viruses to by-pass and effectively hide from oxygen.

By the way, evolutionists believe viruses developed on Earth before cellular plants produced oxygen, and hence oxygen remains a "recent" poison for viruses. Still, because symbiotically viruses need cells to survive, I can't fathom the paradoxical assertion by evolutionists that viruses came first... hmm ...

Viruses thrive in an acidic bodily environment because acidic blood plasma chokes off free oxygen flow by compressing the red blood cells carrying oxygen.

Conversely, alkaline conditions open up red blood cells like sponges, enabling them to absorb and transport great quantities of oxygen. And when in their preferred acidic, low oxygen environment, viruses more easily bind to cell walls, ready to invade them and plant offspring.

Viruses multiply by dividing, but when dividing, their DNA, again reminiscent of "HAL," from the "2001: A Space Odyssey" movie can metastasize to allow the offspring to better survive obstacles in the immediate environment (for example, better avoiding the body's immune mechanisms, or in the case of "HAL" the computer, being able to outsmart Dave, the astronaut).

Most importantly, as the American Cancer Society quote explained, when viruses invade cells, the virus ultimately seeks to destroy or switch some of the cells' DNA, causing its own DNA combo, "hijacking" the cell itself (this book's viral cancer theory). Viruses usually do not get this far. Sometimes they penetrate the cells' outer membrane and are killed off inside of the cell. Occasionally, they make it as far as getting inside of the cells' nucleus where they breed a new hive of viruses, perhaps many thousands of them. But occasionally, as you will see shortly with the virus cancer theory, a single virus "hits a home run" and penetrates the cell's DNA, messing with genes and gene behavioral switches.

But first a look at the spontaneous mutation theory, the theory espoused by most doctors.

Cell Division & the Spontaneous Mutation Theory

We did not discover cell division until the late 1800s. Since then, science determined that the cell goes through multiple staging steps during division.

These include preparation steps *compressing* chromosomes, copy steps *splitting* chromosomes into sister sets, and reassembly steps *building* sister sets up to full-fledged DNA/RNA libraries for their own cell plasma entities.

Given the chemical/sequencing precision needed to pull this off, the chance of what the doctors refer to as a "spontaneous" mutation happening, a screw up, always exists along the way.

Mainstream medicine theories out there stubbornly claim cancer happens when a cell's DNA *mutates in a spontaneous manner during cell division,* but this constitutes naïveté.

Too many thousands of DNA genes and gene switch molecules – the orchestra members – would have to mutate, all in perfect harmony, for the new cancer cell to live. The various thousands of genes, and the vast numbers of switch setting combinations amongst chromosome strands, would require perfect synchronization to keep the emerging cell's biochemical factory operating. Most true mutations result in cell death, as the isolated mutation falls out of step with the vast DNA matrix operating the cell.

The amount of DNA held inside of a cell overwhelms one's comprehension.

Some 20,000 different genes reside within, each gene switched on and off (expressed) via millions of molecular switch combinations.

These switches are like the brail spindle on a player piano activating piano keys. Certain switch molecules activate sets of genes that determine each cell's assigned role in the body (you're a skin cell). Other gene switches happen in real time, as the cell spars with the survival circumstances that it encounters – such as hunger, oxygen depletion, toxin and stimulant absorption, hormonal commands or viral invasions.

Though we hold around 20,000 genes, with each gene a formula for making a specific protein, gene switches rule higher, activating or suppressing one or more genes at any given instance. The gene switching molecules are the true decision makers of the cell, with the genes simply creating RNA orders going out into the cell.

Millions of gene and gene switching combinations would take place if the whole system operated randomly or spontaneously.

Instead, the millions of gene switching molecules - also inherited, and which take up 90% of the DNA string – are just as correlated in their logical relationships as the genes themselves, and if destabilized by random mutation, the cell would "crash and burn" without this kind of air traffic controller cohesion.

For more on this, read the recent reports coming out of the ENCODE project, researching the human genome.

More so, in the face of the above, even if *spontaneous synchronized mutations across DNA strands* could even occur in a single cell, they would have to occur over and over again <u>in the exact manner across the entire human population</u> to result in, for instance, a particular breast cancer type called Estrogen Sensitive Cancer that 70 percent of breast cancer patients contract.

For one to intellectually hold onto *universally identical mass mutations happening "spontaneously" amongst all beings across the vast human species* ... as the root cause of estrogen sensitive breast cancer ... constitutes conceptual folly.

But the Hartford breast surgeon claimed *spontaneous mutation* as the root cause of Laura's condition while we sat in his office. And the best schools in America trained him to say so.

This stunned me as it left his lips, and I remain stunned.

And so, if one dismisses *spontaneous cancer eruption across one out of every eight woman in America as the root cause of breast cancer,* then one instead has to envision a specific agent that causes a good specialized cell, like a lung, prostate, colon, or breast cell, to have its DNA altered right under its very nose.

I'll now offer a more plausible explanation.

The Viral Theory of Cancer

Gazillions of viruses exist everywhere, laying siege to every plant and animal on earth, constantly invading cells, looking for new homes in which to flourish and multiply. Organic beings, such as humans, have two lines of defense to fight off these viruses: the cell's immediate response, and the body's "search and destroy" immune system squads.

For example, the cell initiates chemical responses to blunt the virus's attempt to penetrate, blocking the "receptors" on the cell wall membrane to which viruses attach themselves.

If a virus is tricky enough to penetrate the cell's membrane, the cell has "personal bodyguard" proteins that identify alien threats, with other cell proteins coming in to crush the poor virus just caught.

If the cell cannot keep up against the onslaught, a single virus out of thousands may make its way to the center of the cell where it penetrates the nucleus membrane housing the cell's precious DNA/RNA library.

Once inside the nucleus, the virus takes over – similar to a bank robber – directing RNA to go out into the cell factory and construct a bunch of SPECIAL "viral" proteins and bring them back into the nucleus.

Inside the nucleus, the proteins assemble into thousands of "lifeless" viral drones, á la "Star Wars," sitting dormant inside of the nucleus chamber.

Once the drones are built, duplicated viral DNA strings from the original perpetrating virus fill the assembled drones to bring them to "life"... err, rather, "activity."

And while building a new army of, say, 20,000 viruses (the usual outcome), the perpetrator virus may attempt to infiltrate the cell's DNA, making the cell itself cancerous.

Ugly, but it happens some of the time!

Let's consider the HPV virus. Worldwide, HPV is the most common sexually transmitted infection in adults; more than 80 percent of the world's women (3 billion women) will have contracted at least one strain of HPV by age 50. Most of the 3 billion women infected with HPV will *not* have complications from the HPV *virus*, as "only" 275,000 per year die of related HPV *cancer*, around 0.9 % of the infected base.

This gives one an idea on the rarity of a virus to get as far as to actually cause cancer. But some do.

The Viral Theory Elaborated

Mechanically, viral DNA "strands" consisting of hundreds of synchronized genes and gene switch molecules already working in concert within the virus - are simply infused, wholesale, into the cells DNA, probably during cell division. This is similar to replacing one management team with another after a corporate, political, or military takeover.

When DNA infusion transpires, a normal, "assigned" cell ("assigned" to do a job, such as performing as a lung cell) is no longer switched to operate according to the rules of cell specialization and programmed death/division (ignoring die commands). It is now a cancer cell.

These "cancer cells" do not die, and they can suddenly metastasize, that is, change forms, such as when breast cancer turns into bone cancer. In addition, cancer cells hate oxygen and love acid, just like viruses. All the behavioral elements of cancer comprise the very traits of viruses.

The ability to metastasize must be rooted in the ability of all cells to copy switch settings during cell division. With metastasis, instead of copying one's own settings, the new cell copies another's settings, the way stem cells copy the switch settings of the cell they are replacing.

Of course a well-behaved healthy cell would never copy another cell-type's settings during cell division. Only stem cells and cancer cells copy the configuration of others.

Beyond the cell itself, fighting alone night-and-day to survive, the body brings its massive immune system to bear to kill off viruses skulking around in the blood stream, and to kill off any unfortunate cell unable to repulse the viral attack: annihilating the badly infected cell and the whole 20,000 strong viral newborns living inside. When cells become this sick – to the point where they house 20,000 new viruses waiting to explode onto the scene – the debilitated cell releases last-gasp "S.O.S." molecules into the blood stream.

These "scented" molecules attract outside immune system cells like T-cells or Killer Cells to come in and do the dirty work of killing off the infected cell. Let's call it "assisted suicide."

Good riddance!

So if viruses continually bombard the body, then why doesn't everyone have cancer?

The answer: everyone *does* have cancer, but most bodies, especially younger bodies, possess the strength to keep the viral assault in check.

The body functions as a garden, where daily weeding must take place to keep it from, well, "death by weed."

In the case of cancer cells, if the body does not destroy errant cells in a timely fashion, they multiply unchallenged and form tumor colonies first in the thousands, then in the millions, then into the billions, and even into the *trillions* of cells.

The isolated immune system cells flowing through the blood and lymph systems cannot keep up with the explosion of multiplying cancer cells.

The budding tumors initially feed off of the tiny blood and lymph *capillaries* feathered among the healthy cells from whence they came, but as the tumors grow, they envelop major blood and lymph *vessels* to co-opt voluminous sources of nutrients, squeezing out the healthy cells. And then it's off to the races!

At some point cancer cannot be stopped. It consumes all of the nutrients of the body until the victim suffers emaciation at the cellular level, and finally expires of starvation and oxygen depravation.

You might find the following study enlightening regarding viruses and their obsession with the DNA within host cells …

Retrovirus Theory on Cancer

A research report titled: *Roles of Endogenous Retroviruses in Early Life Events* published by *Trends in Microbiology* describes how viral DNA sometimes becomes implanted within the DNA library of sperm and egg cells. While most viral attacks on cells come and go, the researchers believe that over millions of years, some viruses attacking sperm and egg cells manage to permanently plant their DNA inside of these reproduction cells so that the virus's DNA gets passed along as part of the species it successfully invaded. Examination of human DNA points to around 100,000 such cases of viral DNA tucked away within our cells. Though not much is known of the role of foreign DNA in our everyday lives, this research presents compelling evidence that viruses routinely penetrate our DNA libraries and trigger cancers.

Also before moving on, please consider yet another theory on how cancer starts.

Stem Cell Theory of Cancer

A theory on cancer cites deformed stem cells. Like other cancer theories, damaged DNA is involved, but with the stem cell theory the cancerous DNA is not formed by mature cells during cell division, but inside immature stem cells living amongst the mature cells.

According to the stem cell theory, DNA perversion inside a stem cell causes it to blast out an endless string of "daughter" stem cells that build into tumors. The daughter cells do not multiply; they simply do not die. If this theory holds, it means that each incident of cancer has two different cell types: blaster cells and daughter cells, each possibly needing separate protocols to control. The blaster cells, though, must consume vast amounts of sugar (glucose) to generate this kind of output.

The theory begins with all adult cell types in the body – lung, breast, colon, skin, blood, etc. - having immature "tissue-specific" stem cells living amongst their mature counterparts. This way, if mature cells are damaged, the nearby tissue-specific stem cells can come out of their dormant state and quickly matriculate into a mature state, thereby replacing the damaged cells. Under normal conditions, tissue-specific stem cells are to remain dormant until needed.

The stem cell cancer theory claims that rather than staying dormant, perverted stem cells go on a wild "blaster" reproduction streak, with daughter off springs causing the build up of tumors. Even if one surgically removes the tumor, but does not kill the rouge, proliferating blaster stem cells, the tumor will grow back.

OK, now that we *might* know what we're up against, what's next?

PART III –
MORE UPs and DOWNs

Chapter 7 – Detoxing with Biological Dentistry

As noted a few chapters ago, the time came for Laura and I to meet the Biological Dentist. Before this meeting, beside everything I just explained in the preceding chapters, I deciphered the following about Biological Dentistry itself.

Fundamentally, Biological Dentists believe that disturbances in the mouth (the top anchor of the Energy Meridians), and oral bone bacteria are more harmful to one's health than mainstream dentistry realizes … or understands.

I find it funny the way mainstream dentistry makes a big deal about gum disease: how microbe toxins in the gum enter the blood stream and cause conditions such as hardening of the arteries and heart disease. Yet for some reason mainstream dentistry does not even want to consider that bacteria colonies incubating inside old root canals might secrete other toxins into the bloodstream, enabling cancer. Biological Dentists swear by this last proposition.

They reason as follows: With root canals, the practitioner digs out the main canal and back fills it with a sealant. Before the implementation of this procedure, the main canal, while still alive, feeds thousands of tiny, microscopic side fibrous channels that carry nerve, blood, and lymph support to the whole inner tooth (you probably did not know this).

By carving out the main channel, the root canal procedure "kills" the tooth outright – there on the spot – separating all of the side provisioning fibers from the main canal. The strategy supposes that even in a dead state, the tooth's dense bone will remain in the jaw and not decay, giving one use of the tooth as if it were still alive.

Biological Dentists cite a few things in response:

1. How long do you really expect a dead tooth wedged in your jaw not to create problems? Root canals are a recent phenomenon and the jury remains out on unforeseen, long-term consequences.

2. The canal sealant eventually gets old and shrinks enough to form pathways for micro bacteria to slither into the tooth. They multiply and form colonies inside the abandoned side channel.

3. Every time one bites down, toxins from these bacterial colonies get squeezed out and swallowed, spreading through the body. In turn, saliva is sucked in, bringing needed nutrients back to the bacterial colonies. Whereas gum disease toxins affect the heart, Biological Dentists believe that tooth disease toxins affect soft tissues like breast tissue.

4. Even if the body can tolerate the toxins (many people fare well with root canals), still, because the Life Energy Meridians all end up in the mouth, root canals can also impinge energy supplies down the line.

OK, great, I get the theory. I explain the topic to Laura and off we go on another highway to meet the Biological Dentist - to hear his ideas in the specific case of Laura's #3 & #4 teeth. Perhaps her long lasting #3 tooth infection years ago generated the toxins that made her breast tissue vulnerable to viral cancer.

The 90-minute drive to the dentist offers a somber ambiance. So far, our "journey down the yellow brick road" has made us quiet people. But on the drive down, we discuss where we are, and project what might come of the upcoming Biological Dentist meeting.

The Biological Dentist proves an interesting man. A former Air Force dentist who must have a lot of scientist in him, enough science to try and find what works on a repeated basis, and if it works, to run with it even if the reasons why it works remain, at least currently, theoretical.

He named his thriving practice *Whole Body Dentistry*. At one point, the American Dental Association (ADA) spent seven years trying to shut him down due to his views on mercury fillings, root canals, etc., all of which counter ADA policies.

We stayed there for hours. After presenting our current situation and our *Self-Healing Protocol* framework, he started by taking a sample of Laura's plaque, which we all examined under a microscope and observed the world of bacteria alive in the mouth.

He specifically drew the sample to hunt for specific "bad" bacteria types, stemming from tooth and bone infection.

He next took a panoramic x-ray of Laura's entire jaw to see where issues from the past might still remain. They appeared evident only in teeth #3 & #4, just as we told him.

He recommended removing the #4 tooth treated with a root canal one year earlier. We expected this and agreed to do it, later, however, changing our minds.

VOLL Testing

Then the interesting stuff started, the testing for toxins in the body: heavy metals, pesticides, chemical pollutants, bacterial by-products and funguses. He used a VOLL system, something I had researched on the Internet, yet something I saw severely ridiculed by all Internet commentators ... yet never explained.

Here is the theory behind the VOLL device...

The VOLL machine, a custom computer apparatus, sends low voltage electricity through one's body to measure resistance caused by chemicals buried in the body (one cannot feel the electrical current). It includes a brass pointer, wired from the computer's sending side and a brass pipe wired to the returning side.

The procedure pokes the pointer into one hand of the subject while he or she holds the returning pipe in their other hand, creating a circuit, starting with the computer, flowing through the body and returning back to the computer. A "clean" electric current (at a very low voltage) delivered by the pointer rod easily makes its way through the body to connect up with the receiving pipe held by the other hand.

Next, now that a clean circuit passes through the body with minor, yet measured resistance, the clean current is infused with "electronic spectrum" imprints of various carcinogens. "Spectrums," means the electrical manifestation of a discrete subject, such as Mercury or Fluoride.

Elements and such each have specific electrical spectrums. Sounds, for example, have spectrum shapes we store on compact discs as "music."

Every discrete "thing" out there possesses a unique electrical spectrum; the way every snowflake falls unique.

When we add one of these toxic spectrum images into the clean current passing through the body, the augmented current slows down by resistance provided by actual toxic matter in the body pulling the electronic spectrum toward it.

If, for example, we add the electronic spectrum for mercury to the electrical current entering the body, and real mercury exists in the body, perhaps derived from one's mercury fillings and consuming certain fish over a lifetime, then the electrical current slows down based upon the degree of real mercury it encounters. A high level of contaminant mercury in the body will virtually stop the current in its tracks. The VOLL machine shows the decay in current, which signals the magnitude of the toxin in the body.

A Five-Step/Five-Month Detox Program

The outcome of this benchmarking step became a five-month program to rid Laura's body of deeply imbedded toxins, one class of toxins at a time.

Month One would target respiratory pollutants, Month Two at ingested heavy metals, and so forth.

To achieve these month-long cleansings, the doctor imprinted electronic spectrums of the toxins into a vial of water – not unlike imprinting a CD – telling Laura to take a capful of this augmented water each day. He did not put real mercury into the water, just the electronic spectrum of mercury.

To get a grip on this, just as the Earth's gravity pulls on the moon, one should understand that the moon, too, possesses gravity and pulls upon the earth at a reduced level... but *pull* it does.

Likewise, the mercury image inside of the water, tiny though it may be, nevertheless pulls on the *real* mercury imbedded in the body, and the energy image DRAWS THE PHYSICAL MERCURY OUT!

Hmm ... we will have to digest this claim.

Upon concluding the Biological Dentistry episode, Laura and I drive home, emotionally shattered.

Just *what* had we conjured?

On the way home, we stop en route in Waterbury, Connecticut for dinner at Diorio, a wonderful Italian restaurant I frequented over the years. I remember that we ordered sautéed Broccoli Rabe and Caesar salads ...that we sat, quietly ... and that finally we conversed, trying to assimilate what we had just heard from the Brave New World of Homeopathic Medicine.

Homeopathic Medicine simply means using the same "homeo" substance as medicine that one is going after as the cause of the suffering "pathic." Like cures like. Many incorrectly apply this phrase to all naturalistic and organic cures.

One other thing... the Biological Doctor gave us the phone number of Dr. Robert Bard, a Diagnostic Doctor in New York City who could get a three-dimensional picture of Laura's tumors using a special sonogram system. This would allow us to follow the growth or the retreat of the tumors in great detail.

Dental Hygiene

The Biological Doctor had made a deep impression in regard to the degree of exposure the body has to viruses and bacteria residing in the teeth, jaws, and gums. As mentioned, we had examined samples taken from Laura's mouth under his microscope so that he could gauge the intensity of microbe activity, and look for specific bacteria that do not belong in the mouth.

At home, we ramped up our dental hygiene program to a three-step process: *Electric Tooth Brush* (to clean exterior areas), followed by *Flossing* (to break up microbe colonies between teeth and below the gum line), followed by *Water Pick Cleanse* (to flush everything out, sending it all down the drain).

This proved a no-brainer. Removing billions of microbes from one's mouth on a daily basis enables the immune system to focus on other body zones.

Toxicity and Water

Another thing that really sank in after meeting the Biological Dentist: addressing toxicity in the body begins with an understanding of *water*.

Considering that cells themselves comprise mainly water, that same water probably constitutes more than 70 percent of the human body.

Every toxic element inside your water supply finds its' way to each of the trillions of cells in your body. The water one drinks, proves critical toward keeping the body's cells contamination free.

When we got home from the visit, after looking toxins in the eye vis-à-vis the Doctor's VOLL machine, we immediately switched to bottled water that boasted a clean lab report.

I also read the Doctor's book, *Whole Body Dentistry*, which revealed other key facts, such as…

Over decades, we inhale Mercury molecules millions of times from the mercury vapors escaping from our dental fillings, and we ingest Fluoride, another toxin that we foolishly drink with our water.

These toxins, after years of consumption, stay buried deep inside of us. The crazy thing? Both Mercury and Fluoride are poisons, yet we go out of our way to ingest them on a perpetual basis.

With Mercury, besides dental fillings, carnivorous fish – such as swordfish – contain large quantities of it. Every species of fish ingests some Mercury, as, over time, modern society continues to discharge significant levels of Mercury into the water supply. Ground-feeder breeds such as sole and flounder ingest the least amounts of Mercury. Medium-sized fish eating these smaller fish ingest the ground feeder's Mercury, accumulating higher levels.

Larger fish that eat the medium fish collect even more Mercury concentrations, and so on. At the top of the food chain, Swordfish, for instance, contain 40 times the Mercury, as do the ground feeders.

Moving on to Fluoride, we mix it in with our drinking water to fight bacteria in our mouths, which means that it reaches every cell in our body… just to find the teeth. This crazy practice started after World War II, and later stopped all over the world… *except in America!*

According to the Centers for Disease Control (The CDC), 210 million Americans, out of an overall national population of 313 million, still ingest fluoridated water daily.

And these constitute only two of many carcinogens to which we remain exposed. The Biological Doctor has electronic spectrums for *500* known toxins.

Immune System Empowerment

Toxicity exists *everywhere*, but there *is* good news. If you have lived 40 or 60 years, your body has 40-to-60 years of absorbed toxicity hidden away, BUT you can more or less return to Square One – the way your body arrived at birth – via comprehensive detox efforts.

Laura did the 14-day enzyme-led detox to get things started, and then did five (5), one-month-each homeopathic, energy-led regimens to remove the deep stuff.

Toxins cause free radicals and are acidic, squeezing oxygen out of the blood stream. Toxins next divert the immune system to chase after them, rather then staying focused on disease at hand. Once detoxification begins – and one starts working with clean dishwater again – one can take additional steps to further boost the body's oxygen levels, its energy levels and the overall vigor of the immune system (described in *PART V – BOOSTING THE BODY*).

Chapter 8 – News... and Bad News

Back home, we receive a call saying that Laura's nutrition report has arrived. We go down to see our Holistic Doctor to learn of the results...

The Nutrition Report

For each mineral or vitamin, the lab report shows where your mineral or vitamin level sits in comparison to the general population.

If, say, your B12 level, as achieved through daily digestion and absorption, resides in the bottom 10 percent of humanity, then you need to start taking B12. The report tells you the dosage needed to get you to up to an adequate level.

Laura ranked low in five areas, and she began to take supplements at home, adding these into her daily intake program. The regiment dictated that she take some supplements at specific times of the day, or before or after a meal.

Laura designed a "when and how much" chart that scheduled both the supplements and the Homeopathic waters. It would soon expand to coordinate the immune system bolstering and cancer-infiltration elements of our budding *Self-Healing Protocol.*

Iodine

A funny thing about the nutrient report... it did *not* include an assessment of iodine.

Iodine deficiency correlates highly to outbreaks in breast cancer. Due to this recognized correlation, iodine must play a role in the healthy operation of the unique female cells (breast and ovary cells) designed to divide during menstrual cycles.

As national author Doctor David Brownstein describes:

The breasts contain the third highest iodine concentration in the body, after the thyroid gland and the ovaries. Iodine deficiency in the breast can manifest as fibrocystic breast disease and breast cancer.

I researched suppliers and purchased an iodine supplement.

The Kineologist handling Laura's energy health did more research and set a moderate dose (too much iodine stresses the thyroid, leading to weakness and fatigue). Iodine is an essential ingredient for provisioning female sex cells, and I attribute this corrected deficiency as one of the contributors to Laura's success.

I propose that a lack of iodine debilitates the specialized female cells, making them susceptible to viral infection and/or DNA perversion during division.

I'm not certain about the following, but I find it compelling: iodine – applied to wounds – kills viruses. Because lack of iodine correlates to increased breast cancer outbreaks, maybe the breast cells ward off viral bugs using iodine.

While researching breast cancer topics, I ran into a corollary finding on male prostate chemistry that you might find interesting. Just as female tissue employs iodine (a poison) to regulate organ health, prostate tissue employs zinc (a poison) - 15 times as much zinc as found elsewhere in the body - to fend of viral and cancerous development within that gland.

The body is tricky, using poisons in a controlled manner to do its bidding.

First, the _Good_ News: 3-D Sonograms

Our date for the 3-D Sonogram trip to New York City came up (not to be confused with the other NYC trip to see the Columbia Laser Doctor scheduled a week later).

Dr. Bard, the 3-D Sonogram Pioneer and Breast/Prostate Cancer Specialist, administered the sonogram in the normal manner, with the difference that it dispersed 120 discrete sonogram waves into different depths of the breast and wrote each deeper image to disk.

Back in the doctor's office, a software package, written by General Electric, assembled the different depth images and compiled a 3-D image of the tumor, and the 3-D image could spin around for examination of each side of the tumor.

Two things came of this: a) we now had precise measurements of both tumors; their lengths, widths, and depths, to serve as our baseline, and b) the doctor commented that no big blood vessels entered either tumor, so that the tumors would not have the nutrients to become aggressive in the short term.

He did point out that the large tumor was approaching a vessel, and if it could grow around the vessel, then it would co-opt it, launching an aggressive growth phase.

We left feeling confident that we could go all-out with the diet/cleansing approach, along with all the other measures I came up with, and put off standard surgery for now (though we still held interest in the laser idea).

We made an appointment to have the tumors measured again 10 weeks hence.

And Now, The Big Letdown...

I have not really brought this up until now, but stress, fatigue, and worry do not well serve people trying to arrest cancer.

When in distress, your body's nervous system puts everything on high alert. You assume the classic "fight or flight" stance. At this point, your body's immune and repair systems effectively become shuttered until the body broadcasts certain "all clear" hormones throughout the blood stream, directing cells to finally "rest and recover."

I will discuss the *"Flight or Flight"* versus *"Rest and Recovery"* topic further in the *Boosting Energy* chapter.

I only bring up the role of stress now to put the following event in context: The Columbia Presbyterian Laser Therapy option proved a washout, with heavy fallout on Laura's "psyche."

As I mentioned, I spoke to the Columbia doctor's office multiple times, attained an appointment date, and had all MRIs, Regular Sonograms, 3-D Sonograms and Mammograms sent to the doctor's office, as well as the pathology slides (the actual cancer cell samples from the original biopsy) held at Hartford Hospital.

Laura and I discussed many times that we should not get our hopes up, as the "Laser Zapper" treatment (as we called it) remained experimental, and we might not be wanted. Still, we had mailed in all of our stuff, plus I had contacted their office one day earlier to ensure that they had everything they wanted from us.

And then the big day arrives, and we drive almost three hours into Manhattan to get the lowdown. We leave early and stop for "salad" along the way, and again promise each other not to raise our hopes up too high. We realize that if things do not work out, then "… it's a long ride home."

We arrive. We park. We find the office. They appear embarrassed to see us, saying they tried calling (while we were driving) to say we "… did not qualify."

Besides Laura's 9 mm tumor, the smaller 4 mm tumor existed, and the "funded" research program only considered single tumor cases.

I stayed calm, but knew Laura began to crumble...

Then it all became surrealistic.

They next told us that even if Laura qualified with a single tumor, that their research program still required – get this – 1) a standard lumpectomy to examine the dead tumor zapped by the laser, and 2) a full six weeks of radiation... just in case.

"*Who would sign up for this?*" I asked, and they replied that so far 23 women *had*... The volunteers gained no advantage personally; they did it to help the program.

Apparently research funding for the program came with the lumpectomy/radiation strings attached, until a FDA type of government authority sanctioned the procedure. The procedure itself, they told us, showed results. Their process destroyed 23 tumors without collateral damage to the breast.

Ironically, the collateral damage only came later with the lumpectomy and radiation that the program demanded to protect its own agenda.

They apologized, again, for not making all of this clear during the previous and various phone calls, and asked if we wanted to sign up for a regular lumpectomy.

Our reply?

"*No thanks.*"

Back in the elevator, back in the parking lot, paying for the parking, driving past the George Washington Bridge ... and Laura continues to slowly crumble...

We keep talking to deflate her anger and stress, but it remains a three-hour ride home.

Now, at least, it became official. We would stand on our own. NO MEDICAL INTERVENTION CRUTCHES!

This resolution, though, means digging deeper into the body's biology, and charting our own strategies... without regret.

A "Regular" Dental Visit

But first, one more topic requires attention before we solidify our cancer protocol direction: the idea of extracting Laura's #4 root-canalled tooth.

Laura complains of pain emanating from the bridge attached to teeth #4 and #2 (#3 had been pulled eight years prior).

We assume the pain comes from the #4 tooth, which underwent a root canal one year earlier.

But we were wrong.

Our regular dentist poked around and determined the pain came from tooth #2, a supposedly *good* tooth. He took an x-ray of tooth #2 that revealed no evidence of any issues whatsoever, though the tooth still hurt.

We drilled the bridge down to reduce contact pressure and left it at that, though months later Laura still felt moderate pain coming from tooth #2.

Considering all of the moving parts to Laura's health puzzle, we decided to do nothing with the teeth for now. Instead, we would concentrate on shrinking the tumors.

If the teeth proved part of the root cause of the cancer almost a decade ago, then we would decide upon this at a later time, after we successfully arrested the cancer.

We canceled the #4 tooth extraction procedure agreed upon back in the biological dentist's office, and ignored the tooth #2 pain …for now.

Ok, now let's shrink some tumors.

PART IV
DIET & DIGESTION

Chapter 9 – How Diet Issues Enable Cancer

As said in the book's introduction, three principle rails traverse the self-healing path: *diet* (deprive the cancer of sugar, while nourishing all of the body's good cells); *empowerment* (free the immune system from toxins and then boost its energy level), and *infiltration* (poison the tumors).

Here in *Chapter 9*, we will conceptually explore how diet works, with an outline of the specific diet explained later in *Chapter 10*.

Chapter 9 will prove a long chapter, but I fill it with important physiological and biological elements, including frameworks on digestion, stimulants, fats, nutrients, sugars, toxins, and more.

Let's start with a look at digestion itself: starting with food eaten and excreted through the "digestive tract," followed by a synopsis of how the body processes food once inside the blood stream – and what can happen once this system becomes either flawed or overextended.

Digestion in a Nutshell

Because our biochemical cell factories interact with molecules and not directly, say, with carrots or chicken nuggets, our bodies must break down the things we eat to the molecular level to provide value in the world of cells.

A carrot gets broken down in stages, starting with one's teeth and saliva. Then stomach acids, duodenum bile and pancreas enzymes bombard it ... all before it enters a 22-foot-long small intestine where "good" microbes break things down further.

Inside of our intestines trillions of good bacteria reside, ingesting all of the food sent their way. Once ingested, the bacteria's "body" churns the incoming food and excretes it. The excreted molecules are more refined than the source molecules, allowing absorption through the intestine walls into the blood stream. Also, the bacteria excrete special molecules, like vitamin B12, that our bodies need.

It is hard to accept, but there are many times as many digestive bacteria in our colons then there are cells in our entire body!

Once reduced through this elaborate chemical and bacterial assembly line, nutrients finally enter the blood stream through the small intestine walls, with anything not absorbed passed on through a valve to the large intestine for excretion. Great!

Absorbed nutrients next flow directly to the liver, which converts the nutrients into even finer molecules – ready for cellular uptake – before transporting them by a vein to the heart. From the heart the nutrient laden blood passes through the lungs and is sent back to the heart again via a different valve, and from there the heart pushes both nutrients and oxygen to the body's cells.

Yikes! That's a lot of trouble to go through for a carrot or a chicken nugget! Who made this wacky system up?

To provide perspective on the effort the body exerts to break down ingested food, consider this: Generally, most people ingest two-to-four quarts of food and drink per day, yet the body injects an additional eight quarts of "digestive fluids" into the digestive tract to move things along and break the food down.

We swallow one to two quarts of saliva per day.

Stomach acids contribute another two-to-three quarts, The duodenum receives two quarts of liver-created bile and pancreatic enzymes daily,

And the small intestine weighs in with two more quarts of "lubricant" fluid.

The blood and lymph vessels entwined around the small and large intestines reabsorb almost all of the 10-14 quarts of fluid – both ingested and bodily supplied – leaving only a subset of fluid actually excreted (sweat and kidney filtration actually maintain fluid equilibrium inside the body).

The digestive fluid basically comprises a closed-end system, orchestrated by a strong liver, able to scrub all of the incoming digestive fluids and recycle them.

Stimulants ... Bypassing Digestion

Cocaine, for one, need not pass through these hoops. Once snorted, it passes through nasal membranes inside of the nose and enters the blood stream directly, rushing instantaneously to the brain.

White sugar, caffeine, and alcohol also bypass the standard hoops. Similar to cocaine, we foist these upon the body without digestion's filtering channels.

Once swallowed, they arrive already in the "broken down" micro-molecule form, and the blood stream quickly absorbs them whether or not the body even wants more sugar, caffeine, or alcohol. Direct access to the blood stream remains the trait of all (let's call them) "power bar" substances.

And once "power bar" substances enter the blood stream, internal organs and every single cell undertake the job of purging these unwanted substances from the body. Unwanted "power bars" do not simply proceed to the large intestine similar to other unwanted "visitors".

Instead, now that the "power bar" molecules reside within, they grow into a big, complex deal, creating a rippling effect throughout the system.

Something like brown rice is quite the opposite.

Inside the rice's inner kernel resides a bit of carbohydrate, minerals and vitamins that the body actually wants, but seven fibrous sheaths enclose the inner kernel.

The body works hard to dig through the seven layers and in the process of digging, ONLY THE MOLECULES WANTED BY THE BODY ARE ISOLATED FOR ABSORBTION ... including the rice's *soluble* fiber, its minerals, vitamins, and some of its inner kernel energy.

Actually, the body does not want most of the rice – including its <u>non</u>-soluble fiber – yet even this plays a role by binding with other unwanted food, and by scraping against the intestine walls … a sanitation truck clearing your "street."

Now, take white rice. All seven layers of fiber were stripped bare, leaving a bleached inner kernel, itself stripped of many key mineral and vitamin molecules, leaving almost pure carbohydrate molecules for the body to encounter.

Once inside the system, the body quickly breaks down carbohydrates into sugar molecules, which get absorbed unconditionally, similar to a "power bar." All that remains? Unwanted sugar, but no vitamins or minerals… only clogged intestines.

This situation itself does not cause cancer, but on a chronic basis, surely it sets the table, nicely.

Let's go into more detail. This way you can converse with doctors, nutritionists, and the other experts you will encounter on your journey…

The Blood and Lymph Circulatory Systems

We posses two circulatory systems: the blood and lymphatic systems, with parallel blood and lymph vessels running throughout the body.

Whereas the heart pumps blood through a close-ended *circulatory* system, the lymph passively "oozes" from each cell into open *one-way* lymphatic pathways.

Simple movements of the body then nudge lymph plasma along through lymph vessels. The slow-moving lymph trickles into the blood stream through yet another valve near the heart.

Note: The lymph system, which clears debris from the body, requires exercise to move things along. Laura's six days per week of formal exercise via the karate program was a key to her success. Massage helps as well.

Why *two* systems?

Basically, blood delivers nutrients and oxygen to the cells in a real-time, no-delay manner, whereas lymph performs auxiliary functions at a slower pace, allowing the blood system to remain focused on moment-by-moment delivery of essential fuels.

The lymph system performs specialty jobs such as collecting waste from the cells, delivering white immune cells to desired locations, and transporting fat (packaged as triglycerides) from the intestines to the blood stream.

Tissue Fluid and Osmosis

Every one of the body's 100 trillion cells has access to both blood and lymph services. These capillaries do not touch the cells themselves, but remain in contact with "tissue fluid" that surrounds each cell.

Through osmosis, cells import and export substances from the fluid chamber, and the blood/lymph membranes do the same import/export dance via osmosis to keep the tissue fluid chamber neutral.

Osmosis – The tendency of a fluid to pass through a semipermeable membrane, thus equalizing the concentrations of materials on either side of the membrane.

An important note: in this osmosis-led mechanism, the cells have no choice in what they absorb.

If alcohol exists in the blood stream, the blood capillary membrane will push the alcohol into the cell's tissue fluid chamber for absorption by the cell to create equal concentrations of alcohol inside and outside of the cell wall.

The cell exports alcohol only when the tissue fluid chamber no longer contains alcohol, i.e., after you drink a lot of water and clear the alcohol from your system.

The same goes for *all* toxins. If they exist in the tissue chamber, the cell will take them in to create parity of the substance inside and outside of the cell membrane wall.

Abusing the system

With the above in mind, consider the multi-cup coffee drinker, where Caffeine flows to all 100 trillion cells...

As the kidneys clear the caffeine from the blood stream, all 100 trillion cells start to push their caffeine back out to the tissue fluid and from there, to the capillaries.

Then the drinker ingests the next cup of coffee and the process repeats itself.

With three to four cups, the body spends much of the day pumping caffeine in and out of all of these cells, exhausting the system.

Stimulants are big "no-no's" with cancer fighting diets. Health wise, cells have much more important things to do – such as killing viruses – than to pump useless chemicals in and out of themselves all day long...

Now that we know what *not* to do – consume caffeine, alcohol, sugar, and drugs – let's visualize the *original* design for the body's performance.

Separate Digestion Steps for Fats/Oils and All Other Nutrients

As already described, digestion of incoming food involves a two-step process: raw ingestion by the mouth, stomach, and duodenum, and chemical alteration of ingested materials by the intestines and liver to create molecules actually usable by the cells.. A lot happens to ready nutrient molecules to attach and then pass through the body's 100 trillion cells.

Whether the food presents a fat/oil (meat) or other (a carrot), the digestion process starts out the same way.

Chewing and saliva begin the process. Next the stomach muscles churn the food, mixing in acids, which convert the raw food into a semi-liquid substance called "chime."

Chime then enters the duodenum, where the gall bladder injects bile (the liver actually creates bile, and stores it in the gallbladder until needed to digest a meal).

Bile, an antiseptic, is interesting first in that it kills the microbes that arrive with the food, and second, bile is super-alkaline, neutralizing the temporary acidity of the chime (remember, the body does not want acid). The pancreas then supplies the duodenum with digestive enzymes, designed to separate fat clumps in the chime and to provide insulin for glucose distribution.

Fat raises a special challenge to the body. Fat tends to clump together and cannot mix with water, with water, our centerpiece, constituting 70 percent of our bodies.

To solve this fat/water conflict, pancreas enzymes injected into the duodenum latch onto fat molecules to keep fat molecules from sticking to each other.

The ability of one animal (man) to live off the bodies of outside animals and plants can be boiled down to this. The digestive track reduces the incoming fat and protein molecules structured for the outside organism into smaller building block molecules that human cells reassemble to suit their own purposes. Animal proteins are broken down into a slew of amino acids, which human cells draw upon to form human protein structures ordered up by human DNA/RNA templates.

Upon leaving the duodenum, the chemically separated fat molecules, proteins and vitamin nutrients enter the 22-foot-long small intestines where what we call "good bacteria" break them down further. This relationship between bacteria in our "gut" and the nutrients we need emphasizes why one must take care not to decimate the good bacteria with harmful drugs, including chemotherapy. Conversely, we often see Probiotics prescribed to nurture the good bacteria.

Strings of blood and lymph capillaries surround the intestine cell walls, waiting to absorb the incoming molecular nutrients pre-digested by the good bacteria.

The fat components, however, remain too big to fit through the red blood capillary membranes, so the more-porous lymph capillaries pick the fat droplets up. All of the other smaller nutrients enter the red blood capillaries and next go straight to the liver for further processing.

Fat goes the other way, through the lymph system. Let's follow what happens to fat...

Processing Fat

Upon entering the lymph system, the separated fat droplets reconfigure to create human triglycerides – fat packets. For example, upon eating some Tuna, the incoming fish triglycerides from the Tuna, first broken down into tiny fat droplets, are reconfigured by intestinal cells for the triglyceride design of the human body.

"Fat," in triglyceride form, stands ready to be metabolized into glucose (sugar) inside of the body. The triglyceride packets drift through the lymph vessels and get dumped into the blood stream (at that lymph/blood gateway near the heart).

The blood stream, in turn, exposes the triglyceride packets to the body's fat cells. The fat cells unconditionally absorb the excess triglycerides, storing them away until told to release them in times of sustained hunger.

Note: fat cells continually absorb unused triglycerides by expanding like balloons.

We have a fixed set of fat cells in our bodies; they simply expand, as necessary, to deal with overloads of triglycerides inundating the body. Around 10% of fat cells die each year, but are replaced with a new 10%.

Because the fat cell count remains fixed, when one removes fat via liposuction, the fat cells in the treated area disappear for good. However, if you continue to overload the system, other fat cells take up the slack in a "Robbing Peter to Pay Paul" manner. Your back, rather than your stomach, becomes fat!

Besides warehousing triglycerides, the fat cells operate as a general storage facility for all kinds of excesses floating around the body, such as toxins.

This combination of fat and toxins sitting inside of fat cells is why when starting a cancer-effective cleanse diet, one needs to follow the diet for as long as it takes (typically two to three months) to "squeeze the stuffing" out of the fat cells, thus eliminating the availability of hidden reserves of fat energy and acidic toxins to the cancer cells.

The Interplay of Sugar and Triglycerides

A related point: when you consume sugar, even fruit sugar, the excess calories from the sugar mean that the body does not yet call out the triglyceride reserves, leaving these fat and toxicity reserves intact, thus delaying the effects of the depravation protocol.

A website called ReduceTriglycerides.com offers some lucid observations upon triglycerides, sugar, and cancer:

If you strictly follow a sugar-free diet, a significant drop in your blood triglyceride level should occur in four (4) to six (6) weeks. Unfortunately, many people actually suffer addiction to sugar, and this includes grains, rapidly broken down into sugar by the body.

Only complete avoidance of all sugar and grains will eliminate this physical addiction.

But for several weeks during the transition, you MUST eat *every* two hours to avoid the symptoms of hypoglycemia.

Remember, cancer cells cannot multiply rapidly without sugar, and that the cells that divide the fastest have the highest requirement for energy.

Yet I am flabbergasted that this simple knowledge – *sugar feeds cancer* – does not prevail as Rule Number One in *any* cancer fight: STOP eating sugar immediately.

Still *More* Bad News About Sugar

Ok, that sends another strong message about sugar, but sugar excess raises another issue: Glycation.

A web of stringy things made out of a molecule called collagen holds our bodies together. We are all spider man! But one wants elastic collagen rather than stiff collagen fibers running throughout the body.

Glycation - a biochemical process that comes on strong with age – combines sugar with collagen resulting in an inert new molecule. As a result, pure collagen's "anti-aging" proteins become depleted throughout the body (in other words, *sugar ages you*).

Your skin wrinkles because the proteins needed to produce skin collagen grow scarce due to bonding with excess sugars.

The same happens throughout the body.

As the anti-aging collagen supply dwindles, muscles become less supple; your arteries grow brittle, and so forth.

One cannot control age, but one *can* eliminate simple sugars, thereby preventing this vitality-producing protein from neutralization.

Ok, all of the above concerned fat: its special digestion path, how the body uses it and stores it, and why sugars prevent the total depletion of fat. More on sugar, collagen, scar tissue and breast density later in the book.

A Note on Sugars and PETScans: With PETScans, radioactive sugar is injected intravenously to circulate throughout the whole body. Generally speaking, there are three types of cells that devour sugar – brain, heart and cancer cells. These then glow on the PETScan monitor due to the radioactive element mixed in with the sugar. Hence cancer concentrations can be found with tumors of .8 cm or greater. This gives one a feel for the sugar appetite of cancer cells.

The Liver

Now we must visualize what happens to all other non-fat nutrients entering the bloodstream directly from the intestines.

After your intestines, the biggest single organ in you is your liver.

It starts on your right side and runs all the way to your stomach on the left, connecting back to the digestive tract via its helper organ, the gall bladder (which the liver provisions with cholesterol-based bile used to help with digestion).

Why is the liver so big?

It does a lot of work... that's why. I read that it performs 500 different functions. It mainly scours incoming blood from the intestines, looking for newly ingested food, enzymes, glucose, minerals, and vitamins, plus circulating triglycerides.

The liver uses the various "B" family of vitamins to refine these raw entities into "bite-sized" nutrient packages that can attach to cell walls.

If the body is not "hungry," the liver stores up the refined nutrients, and then slowly drips them into the bloodstream over the next few hours to keep all 100 trillion cells happy.

The liver also manufactures cholesterol. The body uses cholesterol, a building material molecule, to build cell membranes.

Because we have 100 trillion cell membranes, we need a lot of cholesterol. Besides being the "brick and mortar" of cell membrane walls, the body uses cholesterol to create nerve coatings, and to formulate steroid hormones that direct the body's organs.

Finally, cholesterol helps create bile, injected into the duodenum for digestive purposes.

It's everywhere!

HDL Cholesterol, the good cholesterol produced by the liver, possesses a great deal of protein. LDL Cholesterol (the bad cholesterol) mainly possesses fat.

Triglycerides, mentioned earlier, initially packaged by the lymph system, exist mainly as pure fat packets, readily converted to glucose.

Everyone always mentions triglycerides when discussing cholesterol, and I am not sure why people "officially" bundle them together, other than the fat connection. The body forms and uses triglycerides and cholesterol separately inside the body.

A big payoff of the *Self-Healing Protocol* diet is that it eliminates excess fat throughout both facets of the digestive system – blood or lymph. Hence both LDL Cholesterol (mainly fat) and Triglycerides (pure fat) levels will decline in due course. Laura's Triglycerides dropped from 120 to 43.

Last, the liver serves as a big filter, attempting to identify and remove unwanted toxins from the blood stream. It mixes filtered material with cholesterol to make bile, and pushes it into the bile sac for storage. When the liver injects bile into the duodenum for digestive purposes, the toxins go with it, and work their way down the intestines for excretion.

Poor Diets + Toxins = It All Adds Up

The overall point?

If you abuse your digestive process by flooding your body with stuff it does not want – coffee, fats, refined carbohydrates, raw sugars – then you will constantly work your insides overtime.

The likely scenario? You probably (and unwittingly) subject your organs and your universe of cells to the compromise and challenge of dealing with excesses, thus enhancing their exposure to vulnerability to ever-lurking viruses.

OK, not so good, so let's add toxins into the mix to make things even *worse*.

If food excess itself presents a problem, then consider food excess *plus* toxins. Experts estimate that today, thousands of "synthetically manufactured" chemicals and prescription drugs confront our bodies, chemicals that humans never encountered prior to 1900.

For the most part, toxins are acidic, causing free radicles and lower oxygen levels in the body. What mechanism deals with these ugly, oxygen-robbing poisons residing inside your body?

Well, certainly your liver and kidneys get involved, as they serve as the main filtering and excretion organs dealing with toxins and nutritional waste.

But toxins affect all of the other cells, too. Just as the manner in which the body parks excess Triglycerides inside fat cells, it also begins to park all of the toxins inside other cells… say, inside of breast cells, for example.

The "Osmosis" dynamic comes into play everywhere between the cells and the blood/lymph streams, exchanging both natural and man-made chemicals. Just as the roots of plants mindlessly absorb molecules from the outside world, our cells have no choice but to absorb what surrounds them. And just as alcohol makes one woozy upon absorption, toxic substances make each cell woozy.

Toxic chemicals compromise the cell's fragile biochemical DNA/RNA communication network by inserting multiple, meaningless chemical singles into the mix.

The cell can no longer "think clearly" in how to defend itself against the outside viruses continually pressing against its walls.

And so, with defenses down, the viruses gain entry to the cell, where they do their worst.

Toxic chemical signals also slow down the immune system cells. In its groggy, oxygen-depleted state, the body nevertheless calls upon immune cells to kill more and more virally infected cells.

But alas, the feeble immune cells fall behind, and infected cells remain in play and viruses become emboldened.

In some cases, viral assaults go so far as breaching a cell's DNA library and replacing part of the cell's DNA with viral DNA... giving birth to cancer, with an immune system too "fatigued" to do much about it.

The story then continues with colonies of multiplying cancer cells, visible tumors, metastasizing cells… and the eventual death of the host.

Chapter 10 – The Self-Healing Diet

Given everything discussed, I tell people that diet stands strong as the centerpiece to the *Self-Healing Protocol*, but that does not reduce other elements, such as energy and immune system boosting, to superfluous window dressing.

Twenty-eight years ago, with my first wife, diet (in her case, the Japanese diet) existed as the sole element of the protocol, and this, by itself brought her back to life.

But the understanding evolved. Diet might provide the battering ram, but the other elements deliver the necessary "knock out force" to ensure its impact. More so, the surrounding protocol elements help cure you quickly, and further, the full protocol helps to re-launch you at a top-of-the-line health and beauty level.

Speaking of beauty, once on the diet, Laura began dropping weight, which caused her concern. Would the weight loss keep going until she shriveled down to nothing?

Well, at the five-month mark, she leveled out at 113 pounds, the same weight she carried on our wedding day at 28 years of age.

Laura's good friend Audrey, another Black Belt karate enthusiast, maintains the diet at all times, and she does not have cancer.

She just "gets it," and she, too, enjoys "perfect" condition, with "perfect" looks.

Audrey, by the way, helped Laura get started with the diet, showing her where to shop, how to work the juicer, sending us articles, dropping off farm produce, and just providing a steady intellectual and psychological force, always moving things forward. As the song goes: "…that's what friends are for."

The diet comprises three principal considerations:

1. Starve the cancer, primarily by digesting vegetables, thus keeping sugar, carbohydrate, and fat levels as low as possible.

2. Eat foods that produce a more-alkaline, less-acidic digestive responses, as alkaline promotes oxygen, which bolsters normal cells and weakens cancer cells.

3. Make certain your limited food diversity nevertheless keeps you nourished, factoring in the need for vitamins, electrolytes, amino acids, omega 3, and anti-oxidants.

Actually, the diet appears fairly complicated, especially at first, when one must both research and memorize all of the "food rules."

If I wrote this book as a strict diet guide, the diet detail would grow very detailed, very quickly. This chapter will instead cover the basics, so you can quickly gain orientation and take the first meaningful anti-cancer steps ASAP in a week's time.

After taking the basic steps – the steps that deliver 80 percent of the devastating diet effects against the cancer cells – you can read the big, 300-page cancer diet tomes to really get into the fray.

Use incremental information nuggets described in these in-depth books to fine-tune your diet during Months Two, Three, and Four.

Because you will fret as to whether any of this works, you will want to have a few images taken of your tumors along the way to follow the protocol's progress.

Laura had her baseline sonogram taken in Week Three of the diagnosis, with the first checkpoint 90 days out, where they found her larger tumor half of its original size, and the second checkpoint 120 days farther out, at which point they couldn't find the small tumor, and the large tumor reduced by half once more). This kind of result can really keep one motivated.

A Good Diet vs. a "Cancer Diet"

The first thing to understand regarding diet: the difference between a good, *balanced diet* that one might follow if healthy, and a *self-healing diet* wherein one goes to the extra lengths necessary to force advancing cancer back into its hole.

For example, many balanced diets include a portion of fruit… yet fruit contains plenty of sugar… so why include it during the time you endeavor to deny the cancer cells the multiples of sugar they *crave*? Though fruit offers anti-oxidants, supplements can be adopted instead.

Likewise, with acid: acidic blood weakens the body's cells, including immune system cells, depriving them of oxygen. Conversely, cancer cells hate alkaline, as alkaline introduces more oxygen. And so enjoying steak (acidic) must wait until you tame the cancer, and kale (alkaline) must become a dietary staple.

Because you cross off many things you currently ingest and enjoy from your diet, the diet thus poses a daunting challenge, especially early on, when, through habit, comfort, and even addiction, you will crave the foods you must eliminate. Only time, one month, at least, can soften this, so you need to gain the motivation set forth by the prize promised in the title of this book: *Defeating Breast Cancer – Organically, No Surgery, Chemo, or Radiation.*

And, at all times, remember the "sugar and acid" rules: cancer needs many times the sugar as do normal cells, and acid suppresses oxygen.

Acidic Blood

A few chapters back, I explained why lemon juice, though acidic, causes an overall alkaline effect on the blood stream.

Likewise, red meat itself is not acidic; it just causes the stomach to release large quantities of stomach acid in order to break the meat down. The broken down acidic-laden meat (chime) next enters the duodenum, which injects alkaline bile, but not enough to neutralize the overall acid level passing through. Hence, red meat drags higher levels of acid along with it into the intestines, and therefore into the bloodstream. Once inside the bloodstream, meat metabolizes into acidic-leaning molecules, further adding to the acid forming effect throughout the body.

With this explanation of acidic versus alkaline forming foods in mind, the following chart illustrates the ranking of foods tied to acidity/alkalinity, with food rankings further annotated based upon sugar content.

Acid (-) Versus Alkaline (+) Forming Food Rankings - *With Sugar-Laden Foods Italicized*

-4 *Pudding, Jam, Jelly, Sugar, Soda, Ice Cream*, Beef, Lobster, Fried Food, Beer, Antibiotics

-3 *Cranberry*, Coffee, Cottage Cheese, Pork, Veal, Mussels, Chicken, Corn, Peanuts, Carrots,

-2 *Alcohol, White Rice*, Vanilla, Black Tea, Balsamic Vinegar, Cheese, Lamb, Shell Fish, Beans, Tomatoes

-1 *Honey, Maple Syrup, Dried Fruit*, Cream, Butter, Yogurt, Eggs, Fish, Brown Rice, String Beans, Zucchini,

+1 *Oranges, Grapes, Blueberries, Strawberries*, Quinoa, Wild Rice, Seeds, Olive Oil, Brussels Sprouts, Beets, Squash, Lettuce,

+2 *Pear, Apple, Cherry, Peach*, Green Tea, Apple Cider Vinegar, Almonds, Potatoes, Mushrooms, Cauliflower, Eggplant, Lemon

+3 *Molasses, Cantaloupe, Honey Dew*, Soy Sauce, Cashew, Pepper, Garlic, Asparagus, Broccoli, Endive, Grapefruit, Olive

+4 *Nectarine, Raspberry, Watermelon, Tangerine, Pineapple*, Sea Salt, Mineral Water, Pumpkin Seed, Sea Weed, Miso, Sweet Potato, Lime

Please note that sea salt is a +4 and table salt is a -4. This dichotomy exists because sea salt is the very saline solution the body strives for, identical to the ocean. Conversely, when consuming table salt, the body tries to fix this "plain" salt invasion, wanting it to be sea salt. By robbing the blood of molecules to achieve this, the blood is left in an acidic state.

The Mayo clinic claims that this differentiation between table salt and sea salt is unfounded, as both substances are primarily the same, a whole lot of sodium nitrate. But that misses the point. The aspects that are different – the 90 trace elements in Himalayan Sea Salt, for instance – are the very elements the body craves. When missing, the body compensates by drawing internal molecules to the table salt to shore it up. Table salt is a free radicle stealing molecules from the body.

Most of my comments regarding acidic versus alkaline forming foods comes from the research of ELIS/ACT Biotechnologies. Their PDF, "The Alkaline Way Guide" is available on-line.

One more reference, a hamburger, fries and a coke are about as bad as it gets. The hamburger causes acidity and if charbroiled, comes with burnt meat molecules that bind with sugar to increase glycation. The fries are carbs soon to be a sugar spike, cooked in oil causing an intake of bad Omega 6 – which then neutralizes the body's good Omega. The coke causes high acidity and sugar spikes.

Your poor liver cannot regulate all of this. Sugar and acid spikes occur in the blood stream and cancer rejoices.

Chapter 11 – Dietary Supplements

Besides depriving cancer, the cancer diet needs to fully provision all of the other cells of the body, and we achieve this through supplements. *Six* key dietary supplements surfaced: Fatty Acids, Amino Acids, CoQ10… the B vitamin family… vitamin C… and "vitamin" D.

Vitamin A, E and K tilt important as well, but these dwell in abundance inside green leafy plants, which Laura consumed daily.

Supplement #1 - Fatty Acids - Omega 3

Omega 3 is referred to as a fatty acid (found in fats). Omega 3 supplements come from fish and krill oil, and most health professionals advocate supplements of Omega 3 in one's diet to directly enhance many facets of the body and also to counter balance high Omega 6 levels (Omega 3 & 6 need to balance each other out as this balance affects the resolve of the previously mentioned BRCA 1&2 genes – described below).

Omega 3 bolsters the heart, tempers all sorts of mental issues like ADHA, and augments many other aspects of health, but for the purposes of this manuscript, one should be aware of it's role in preventing breast cancer.

Doctor Mercola explains:

Two studies from 2002 explain how omega-3 can protect against breast cancer. BRCA1 (breast cancer gene 1) and BRCA2 (breast cancer gene 2) are two tumor suppressor genes that, when functioning normally, help repair DNA damage, a process that also prevents tumor development.

Omega-3 and omega-6 fats have been found to influence these two genes – omega-3 tends to reduce cancer cell growth, while highly processed and toxic omega-6 has been found to cause cancer growth.

Omega 6 excesses come mainly from certain cooking oils – vegetable, canola, etc. -, and to temper this one should switch to olive oil and butter. We use a unique Omega 3 supplementation that claims to be easily absorbed by the intestines.

Supplement #2 - Amino Acids

The body comprises roughly 70 percent water, with the next largest substance, "protein", at 20 percent of overall body weight. ("Protein" in biological speak means an organic molecule – not meat).

All of the structural aspects of cells, and most of the chemical agents directed by cellular RNA, comprise various configurations of protein. *Amino acids* form the chemical building blocks the body uses to create these varied proteins.

The Digestion chapter described how consumed proteins of animals and plants are reduced to amino acids that the human body re-assembles to make human specific proteins.

Hence, one needs an adequate and constant pool of amino acids running through one's system for the full provision of normal cells.

As described, when we digest proteins such as meat or fish, the digestive track breaks down the source proteins into amino acids, absorbed by the intestines and sent up to the liver for additional processing. Just as the body requires a persistent availability of oxygen supplied by the lungs, the liver releases the amino acids to the heart at a constant rate for continuously availability to all 100 trillion cells.

The cells, in turn, convert the incoming amino acids into the protein required at the moment (not the exact protein found in the ingested chicken).

Although the liver does a good job in spreading out the delivery of amino acids to the body, it can only release as much as given, so …

If one does not absorb enough amino acids due to dietary shortcomings or absorption issues, then all 100 trillion cells become handicapped. This "starvation" phenomenon increases as one ages, and so, amino acid deficiency creeps up on you.

The major amino acids include: Argintine, Carnitine, Glutamine, Methionine, Ornithine, and Taurine. One should read up on each of these to decipher which shortcoming resides behind one's specific symptoms.

For example, the heart muscle particularly requires Taurine. If you have heart issues, perhaps uneven rhythm, you may possess a Taurine deficiency. A good heart doctor can weigh in on trying a very small dose to evaluate any potential relief.

In the case of cancer, a debate rages over Argintine, which affects the circulatory system, enabling blood flow and delivering greater levels of oxygen throughout the body. Proponents say that this boost of oxygen acts as a poison to the cancer tumors; detractors say that enhanced blood flow enhances the nutrient levels reaching the tumor. We added an Argentine supplement to the protocol, as it is oxygen oriented, and anyway, we already deprived cancer cells of sugars.

Another option investigated but also not adopted is CAAT – Controlled Amino Acid Therapy. Here, those amino acids believed to provision cancer cells are eliminated, while other amino acids that boost the immune system are added. This treatment includes a very specific daily diet. The researchers involved claim CAAT works faster to shrink tumors than basic sugar depredation.

Supplement #3 - Coenzyme 10 (CoQ10)

The literature claims that our little friends, the Mitochondria, directly access CoQ10, a coenzyme found in many foods and assembled by the liver, and that the little buggers need it to do their job.

People gain vitality in taking CoQ10, and so, I added a mild dose of CoQ10 to the *Self-Healing Protocol*, once I thought Laura's cells reached detoxification, ready to go.

The Mayo Clinic on CoQ10:

CoQ10 levels decrease with age and may be low in people with cancer, certain genetic disorders, diabetes, heart conditions, HIV/AIDS, muscular dystrophies, and Parkinson's disease. Some prescription drugs may also lower CoQ10 levels. CoQ10 in the body can be increased by taking CoQ10 supplements.

Later, Doctor Bard (The NYC doctor with the 3D sonogram) added his own CoQ10 formula to the protocol, which had more potency.

Supplement #4 - The Vitamin B Family

The Vitamin B family contains eight varieties of B vitamins, including the special B12 vitamin, usually deficient in most of us.

Apparently, these variants of Vitamin B, each in its own way, help the liver to further break digested food down so that cells can absorb the nutrients.

Consumers can find vitamin B complex supplements anywhere, and one should take a modest dose as part of the *Self-Healing Protocol*. Based upon blood nutrition tests, a special B12 supplement could be indicated as well.

When we added Argentine to the protocol, it included the B family, and we used this approach rather than a strict B supplement.

Supplement #5 - Vitamin C

Let's look at C's important attributes.

First, your body does not produce or store "C". It is ingested, "water-soluble", floating through the blood stream, continually purged by the kidneys; so new "C" is needed each day.

Second, "C" is a "reducing agent" meaning it readily donates electrons to "free radical" molecules thereby neutralizing (reducing) these scavengers.

Third, "C" is a great "anti-oxidant". It provides a molecular skin that protects cell walls from exposure to oxygen. It also protects the body's supply of fats, proteins and vitamins floating around from oxidation.

Fourth it is required to make the aforementioned collagen (the body's bungee cords).

Nevertheless, the body can only absorb around 500 MG of C at a time, and mega doses disrupt various systems in the body, such as the digestive track and one's sleep, while also making the kidneys work overtime.

The Mayo Clinic recommends 2,000 units a day, but many would double this when under attack by a virus – so long as it was spread out over the 24-hour cycle.

Laura (and I) stayed with moderate doses of vitamin C and never "caught" a cold. The 1,000 unit Emergen-C product was our weapon of choice, as it delivers "C" as well as electrolytes. Never getting a cold gave me confidence that our cells were well protected against viral attack.

A "C" controversy: For 30 years I've heard claims that cancer thrives in a vitamin C rich environment. Looking into this, all I found was that C blunts the effect of certain chemo treatments. Part of the chemo effect is to expose the tumor to oxygen, and vitamin C shields the tumor from oxygen, as C is an anti-oxidant. But this chemo-specific angle is very different than cancer actually thriving on C. It thrives on sugar.

Supplement #6 - "Vitamin" D

Notice the quotation marks around the word "vitamin". This is due to Vitamin D not being a vitamin; it is a hormonal steroid.

Vitamins like the B's and C, are outside molecules supplied from food, used to build cells, create anti-oxidants, and to metabolize nutrients – vitamins are *externally* supplied "ingredients," if you will...

Hormonal steroids, on the other hand, are *internally* created by the body to cause behavioral responses in cells, such as telling cells to divide, telling cells to die, or telling the brain one is hungry – "cellular traffic cops," if you will. "D" is one of these internally made steroid molecules, though most still incorrectly refer to "D" as an ingested vitamin rather than as a sunlight triggered chemical formation in the skin. "D" works as a systemic steroid, meaning that it affects every cell in the body, working to keep the specialized cell types on course as they divide, e.g., making sure dividing lung cells produce lung cells, hair cells produce hair cells, etc.

The various cell types all have the same set of 20,000 chromosomes. Cells specialize through the already mentioned switch settings governing the chromosomes. A lung cell has the same genes as a liver cell, but specific gene switch settings make it a liver cell.

Stem cells, the exception, start neutral, and have no switches turned off or on. For example, when a stem cell morphs into a muscle cell, it copies the switch settings of a muscle cell.

"D" is a "cheerleader-like" stimulant telling the genes to stay switched. All kinds of "D" receptors reside inside the cell, waiting to talk to "D" so genes can stay reassured as to their proper setting.

When cells are not "reassured," they become "lost," and malfunction, probably resulting in everything from depression to breast cancer to autism.

For instance, according to a Doctor Mercola, a strong link exists between "D" and autism, as follows…

"In more recent years, rampant vitamin D deficiency has been linked to a proportionate jump in autism. While the connection may not be obvious, it's important to realize that vitamin D receptors appear in a wide variety of brain tissue during early fetal development, and activated vitamin D receptors increase nerve growth in your brain".

Researchers have also located metabolic pathways for vitamin D in the hippocampus and cerebellum of the brain, areas that are involved in planning, processing of information, and the formation of new memories. The National Institutes of Mental Health concluded that it is *vital* that the mother get enough vitamin D while pregnant for the baby's brain to develop properly.

My take on Autism is different, though the lack of "D" can be a factor in neurons not being created properly. If "D" were the main driver, Autism would have been around forever. Instead, I propose a new phenomenon inserted into the environment around 30 years ago the trigger of Autism. That intrusion is pesticide coated seeds.

Rather than spray plants from above, the seed itself is coated with pesticides so that the germinating plant carries the poison inside of it. Pesticide poisons are formulated to disrupt the nervous system of the insect feeding off of the plant. This is why bees get lost trying to find the hive after ingesting pesticide-laden pollen.

With modern mothers eating food derived from such plants, enough nerve debilitating toxins reach the fetus, and if also lacking in "D", the confused neurons cannot develop fully.

Ok, back to "D".

The body creates "D" mainly from sunlight penetrating the skin. But many "modern" people do not get enough sunlight and hence not enough "D."

This deficiency descends to every cell in the body, with specialized cells, like brain or breast cells, each negatively affected by lack of "D" in its own "gene-switch-confused" manner.

Your nutrient blood test will measure your "D", allowing your diet specialist to recommend a supplement dosage.

By the way, when under mental stress or exertion, the brain draws down huge quantities of "D," so your standing "D" level needs a built-in reserve.

A report in the *Journal of Neurology* by a Doctor Llewellyn cites that the risk of dementia dramatically increases as one's level of "D" decreases (though I proscribe the pesticide driver here as well).

Likewise, the *British Medical Journal* published findings that for those with a history of breast cancer, lack of "D" increased the chance of getting cancer by 70 percent.

"D" is a must have supplement that affects everything, ESPECIALLY IF THE CELL HAS BEEN WEAKENED BY A TOXIN.

Overall, with "D" and the others, the supplement goal remains to give the cells a supply boost, so that they can execute their functions more vigorously, including augmenting internal cell defenses against viruses, and provisioning immune system cells to fight the good fight against viruses and cancer breakouts.

Take your supplements!

Next... boosting the immune system.

The goal is to keep the immune system focused on cancer. Long digressions when fighting off colds and flu, through the immune assault off track. I just mentioned vitamin A, saying that Laura gets plenty of A via leafy vegetables. Vitamin A provisions the immune cells lying along the respiratory and digestive tracks, so it is vital in holding the fort, so to speak, from external microbes entering the body. Should one feel a cold coming on, this warrants a 2-3-day boost in Vitamin A, D and C. C is water soluble, washed out daily. But D and A are fat soluble, meaning they are warehoused by the body in one's fat cells. Hence one can over do A and D intake. But a couple of day's boost is reasonable. Do not let viral colonies proliferate!

PART V
BOOSTING THE BODY

Chapter 12 – Boosting The Immune System

Because Laura started strong right away with the cleansing and diet tactics, she fundamentally established the pillars of her protocol by Week Four. Now we wanted to strengthen the resolve of her immune system.

We could surely consider *many* approaches to bolster this vast military operation. After a lot of reading, it came down to two supplements: *Red Reishi Mushroom Extract* ... and *Beta Glucan*.

But to appreciate these, one must first peak into the fundamentals of the immune system. Here goes...

Offense and Defense

The functions of the body exist as two main camps Offence & Defense:

The Offense Camp includes the Nourishment/Respiratory functions (eating, breathing, digestion, vascular delivery, liver/kidney filtering and waste disposal). These functions bring in and distribute minerals, vitamins, fats, sugars, amino acids, proteins and oxygen to each of the trillions of cells in the body.

Once the body delivers these, the biochemistry inside each cell (including the aerobic actions of the Mitochondria, described later) blends resources to fuel the cells existence. Mathematically, I cannot say how many simultaneous offensive cellular-level chemical events occur within our gigantic life systems, but I can try.

We estimate that each of our bodies possesses 100 trillion cells, and, within each cell, a million molecular events might occur at any given moment: that's 100 trillion cells multiplied by one million molecular events in concurrent action (let's call it … "a gazillion"). Electric energy packets manufactured by the cell's mitochondria propel these molecular actions… (as promised, more to come on this).

This, then, constitutes the offensive side of the body, the camp driving life forward.

The Defensive Camp

The Immune System Defense Camp comprises the second camp, and the body charges it with "watching the back" of the entire offensive operation.

The "all-defense, all-the-time" Immune System stands as quite an operation in its own right, and rightfully so!

At every moment millions of "microbes" (viruses, bacteria, funguses, parasites), as well as toxins (lead, mercury, pesticides, carbon monoxide, etc.) enter your body. As said in sports, "defense often trumps offense."

Before going into some further detail on how the "defensive" immune system works, just consider what could go wrong with the offensive side of the body if the defensive side lets the invaders get the upper hand.

The answer, death via infection: regardless of whether viral, bacterial, fungus, parasite, or toxic agents drive that infection. This need for a massive defense against a mathematically unfathomable attack by foreign enemies makes boosting the immune system a mandatory strategy toward keeping cancer in check.

Let's look in some detail at how the immune system works.

Immune System Mechanics 101

The Immune System comprises an entire set of specialized cells and protein molecules geared to detect foreign agents and kill them ASAP. One can divide these forces into various specialized units, which, through chemical signaling amongst themselves, formulates an overall defensive shield for the body. I'll provide a high-altitude view of what's going on in the trenches, inside each of these specialty camps...

Antibodies – The Searchers: White blood cells secrete these proteins (antibodies are non-living proteins) which, like snowflakes, come in millions of shapes and sizes. They flow through the body and bump into things, looking for "foreigners," the aforementioned viruses, bacteria, fungi, and parasites.

Each foreigner bears a unique chemical appendage on its surface (think of it as a "lock"). To pick this lock, the millions of unique "antibody" proteins floating around represent potential "keys" to that lock. If an antibody's molecular key happens to line up with the foreigner's lock, then they bind. Scientific language refers to these chemical structures (the "locks" and the "keys") as "Receptors."

Once a match occurs between the respective receptors, the antibody scout (which carries only a whistle, and not a loaded gun) releases another chemical to warn the rest of the immune system that *a bad guy has been identified – backup is needed.* Backup primarily comes in the form of gun-carrying T-Cells, Natural Killer Cells, Macrophages, and Neutrophils.

When none of the millions of antibody receptors in circulation match up with the foreigner's receptor, the foreigner runs wild, undetected, proliferating for days within the body.

The white blood cells must somehow create a new antibody protein whose receptor does match the foreigner's receptor; otherwise, the infection will remain undetected, and will take over and kill the body, one cell at a time.

Sometimes, a key cannot be found, and the invader wins, killing the host (that's you), with viruses such as Ebola or Viral Pneumonia. But most of the time the attacking virus is sought out, marked, and assaulted by various immune agents, as follows:

B-Cells - The Librarians: After all of the effort taken to find a match between the receptor surface of an antibody protein and the receptor surface of a foreigner, the immune system wants to file the new finding away for future reference.

This way, if the foreigner ever comes back, the immune system can forego all of this searching and quickly roll out the exact antibody needed to match up with the foreigner to quickly identify the foreigner for what it is – a foreigner.

This filing system of foreigners and their receptor layouts is the job of B-Cells. B-Cells circle around the blood system looking for antibodies already attached to foreigners, antibodies currently sending out SOS's. The B-Cell copies all of this valuable receptor data down for posterity.

When a B-Cell cannot find work — there are no antibodies SOS-ing for help — it dies, and one's bone marrow releases new B-Cells to start the journey all over again.

BTW, scientifically, medical papers – should you dare to read them - refer to "foreigners" as *antigens*.

When a B-Cell *does* get work, it imprints the receptor layout of the foreign antigen onto itself, and, rather than die, the enlightened B-Cell proliferates (divides) and thereafter secretes antibodies that fit those specific foreign receptors, so that future encounters with that same foreign antigen are quickly deciphered. Go "B-Cells".

That's why it seems that you don't usually "catch" the same flu strain twice (actually, you *do* catch it again, but B-Cells quickly detect it). Go "B-Cells again!

The librarian role of B-Cells brings up the topic of vaccines.

Vaccines proactively allow the body to find and stow the anti-body key to a particular disease within one's B-Cell library. A vaccine contains a chemical fingerprint of a disease-causing microorganism, made from weakened or killed forms of the microbe, its toxins or one of its surface proteins.

The injected fingerprint agent stimulates the body's immune system to find an anti-body that will mark the agent as a threat, and then keep a B-Cell record of it.

Going forward, the immune system can more easily recognize and destroy any of these microorganisms that it later encounters.

It is often said, "without vaccines, mass infections of whole populations would take place."

Yet there is controversy, as many parents have experienced children becoming "feverishly" ill upon vaccination, later finding the child's personality and/or mental abilities permanently altered. According to Doctor Bronstein, "the vast majority of flu vaccines are preserved with a mercury compound called thimerosal. Many vaccines contain other toxic additives, such as the carcinogen formaldehyde". Hmmm …

T-Cells – The Foot Soldiers: Once antibodies "smoke out" the antigens (foreigners), T-cells actually kill foreign antigens (with feeling). Overall, we refer to them as T-Cells because the stem cells from which they originate change into Immune System cells inside the Thymus (T) gland in the neck.

As a footnote: an example of the aging process provides that the Thymus gland produces three percent fewer T-Cells per year once one enters middle age. Yikes, we need all of the "T" cells we can get if we are to live "forever".

Unfortunately, the Thymus gland often produces imperfect T-Cells that cannot distinguish between normal and foreign cells, (very bad cops).

These dangerous T-Cells are usually killed off themselves; if not, they aggressively go after normal cells, hence the "Autoimmune" diseases of Lupus and AIDS. Lupus malfunctions remain a mystery. AIDS, however, is a virus (viruses again!) that has co-opted the T-Cells.

Natural Killer (NK) Cells - Special Forces: NK Cells are another type of white blood cell (coming directly from the bone marrow, not matured by the Thalamus gland) that specialize in hunting tumor cells and viruses (the same thing really if you accept my virus theory of cancer).

Unlike T-Cells, which need antibodies to first flag down the foreign antigens, NK cells "frisk" encountered suspects to find out if the entity carries a "self" marker (a chemical form of proper ID). Should the NK Cells find no evidence of "self" marking, they then bore holes in the foreign entity, filling it with poisons like oxygen (nasty business).

Monocytes & Macrophage – The Mop-Up Squad: These long-living (two month) cells go after dying or infected cells and other "debris" to keep the body clean, thus fostering healing.

A "baby" Monocyte arrives as a junior version of the ultimate Macrophage cell, just coming out of "boot camp" (the bone marrow is the boot camp), so to speak.

But when other immune cells finally call them into action, the immature Monocytes quickly morph into various Macrophage forms, now essentially, "special ops" cells that cater to different tissue type malfunctions throughout the body.

Besides mopping up dying cells, cancer cells, and foreign invaders, the mature Macrophages biochemically direct other immune cells via receptor signals when the "crime site" requires more work.

When out of work, the Macrophage specialists simply "hang out" in nearby barracks (usually in connecting bone joints) and await the next call of duty.

I am not making this up!

Neutrophil – The First Responders: Each day, the bone marrow releases 100 billion Neutrophil immune system cells into the blood stream. They move throughout the body, do their job, and then die within hours of being deployed.

Their job: penetrate every nook and cranny of the body at the capillary level and lie in wait for chemical "SOS" signals – called "chemo taxis" – secreted by any nearby injured or infected cells asking for immediate help.

Neutrophil cells come running, and cause inflammation and puss in the infected area, effectively "holding the fort" until the "big guy" white blood cells can come in to do the heavy lifting.

Once the Neutrophil's short, one-hour life ends after having not found anything, a big Macrophage scavenger cell eliminates the tiny Neutrophils scout (remember, "No good deed goes unpunished…").

Again, I am not making this stuff up.

The preceding provides a flavor of the enormous moment-by-moment, chemically induced operation of the immune system - orchestrated using gazillions of cell and protein receptor match-ups to spur further chemical releases that spur further events – all rigged to kill real foreigners such as bacteria, viruses, fungi, and parasites, and to kill rogue cells that have turned cancerous.

So given all of the effort put forward by the immune system on your behalf, the only thing one might add is the question: *What can I do to help?*

Research turned up the following...

Beta Glucans

Glucans – Glucans, a nutritional molecule that one gets from various foods including grains and mushrooms, appear to help on two fronts – reducing high cholesterol, and boosting the immune system. We like both of these.

On the cholesterol-benefit side, the fibrous nature of Glucans helps inside the digestive tract.

Glucan molecules bind with excess cholesterol molecules, creating an inert substance that the body purges – thankfully - rather than absorbs. Hence the following quote from the European Food Information Council:

Beta-glucan, a type of dietary fiber found in abundance in oats, has been recognized as having blood cholesterol-lowering properties. A major proposed mechanism is that dietary oat beta-glucan forms a viscous layer in the small intestine.

The viscous layer attenuates the intestinal uptake of dietary cholesterol as well as the re-absorption of bile acids (which the body makes from cholesterol). In response, the body draws upon the pool of circulating cholesterol to produce new bile acids. Lower uptake of cholesterol from the gut combined with more bodily cholesterol used for bile acid production results in reduced levels of cholesterol circulating in the blood.

On the immune-system-benefit side, Glucan acts as an "immunomodulation" agent (I often wonder who made this word up), meaning that it heightens the activity of the immune system.

The immune attack cells grow more aggressive, and communication among the specialized immune cells becomes more emphatic, not unlike a basketball team suddenly shifting into "domination mode" on the court.

To give the reader a flavor of scientific writing, consider a few sentences from this research report on Beta Glucans from the 2009 *Journal Of Hematology & Oncology*:

Glucans act on several immune receptors including Dectin-1, complement receptor (CR3) and TLR-2/6 and trigger a group of immune cells including macrophages, neutrophils, monocytes, and natural killer cells. Glucans are captured by the macrophages via the Dectin-1 receptor with or without TLR-2/6. The large glucan molecules are then internalized and fragmented into smaller sized glucan fragments within the macrophages. They are carried to the marrow and endothelial reticular system and subsequently released. These small glucan fragments are eventually taken up by the circulating granulocytes, monocytes or macrophages via the complement receptor (CR)-3. The immune response will then be turned on; one of the actions is the phagocytosis of the monoclonal antibody tagged tumor cells.

This last perhaps undecipherable sentence simply means that tumor cells tagged by antibodies as "foreign" suddenly appear visible to the immune cells, which can now devour (phagocytosis) the tumor.

I keep wondering: How young pre-med people memorize these incoherent descriptions?

And because Glucan comes into the blood stream through digestion, we can easily supplement it by taking Glucan-extract pills.

The body uses what it wants, so having elevated levels of Glucan moving through the small intestine cannot hurt; this simply assures the continuous presence of an ample level to fortify each of the billions of immune cells the bone marrow and the Thymus gland deploy each hour. Take Glucans!

Red Reishi Mushrooms

There is a common understanding amongst humans that mushrooms are "special", though few know why this might be so.

The world offers many varieties of mushrooms, and many offer valuable nutrients not readily found elsewhere. But the *Red Reishi Mushroom* sits atop the heap among the many with its various "active agent," molecules that dramatically affect cells in the human body, including offering its own unique glucan molecule.

Very notable: Red Reishi pushes immune system cells to attack "impenetrable" tumors, and not just "tiny" viruses and bacteria. Scientifically, I do not know why this is so, but many, many health practitioners claim that it is so.

Where are the young, driven PHD candidates on this topic?

In Eastern Medicine, for 2,000 years, doctors who cared for the Oriental Royal Families prescribed Red Reishi, initially rare and difficult to accumulate, as it only grew in a natural setting on certain decaying tree trunks.

But recently the Japanese finally found a way to cultivate it in greenhouses, with its extracts now available in pill form (thank-you Japan). Other Reishi species exist, but the red ones remain the "cat's meow" as far as the immune system goes.

Some also use Red Reishi for high blood pressure and other ailments. *Natural News* describes Reishi as follows:

Research shows that the polysaccharide beta-1,3-D-glucan in reishi boosts the immune system by raising the amount of macrophages and T-cells. This immune-boosting action works wonders in the prevention and treatment of cancer. In addition to boosting immune system numbers, the glucan in reishi helps immune cells bind to tumor cells. Another substance in reishi, called canthaxanthin, slows down the growth of tumors. It directly reduces the number of cancerous cells, making it easier for T-cells and macrophages to rid the body of them. Research and traditional medicinal usage of reishi to fight cancer is so positive that the Japanese government officially recognizes it as a cancer treatment.

I find that paragraph about as lucid a "medical school" paragraph as one might find while researching these sorts of things, and so I included it here. Most scientific writing contains so many Greek and Latin words framed in obtuse medical jargon, that one holds little or no chance of understanding it unless one goes all out for days on end to solve the word puzzles and obtain context.

Still, I recommend that you dig into medical studies on all kinds of things and grow accustomed to the babble! Deciphering medical babble changes your mind from that of passive accepter of medical intervention authority to active prospector of new knowledge, a mindset that dovetails beautifully with the *Self-Healing Protocol.*

Other research uncovered the following about immune cells…

1. Immune system breakdowns – like Crone's

Crone's disease, named after Dr. Crone who first described the condition in the early 1900's, occurs when one's immune system mistakenly attacks good bacteria in one's intestines, creating vast amounts of inflammation both in the intestines and throughout the whole body. Why the immune system is fixated on killing the good digestive bacteria is unknown.

A possible construct to explain Crone's comes back to viruses. In this theory (my theory), the viruses in question do not invade the body's cells, but instead infect the trillions of bacteria living symbiotically inside of one's digestive track. The infected bacteria nevertheless attract bodily immune scouts looking for foreigners (antigens), and instead of creating antibodies identifying the virus, the immune cells "mark" the sickly bacteria as the problem.

Once catalogued as trouble by the librarian "B" cells, the immune attack cells target the innocent bacteria in the intestines, filling the intestines with inflammation in an attempt to stem the "perceived" enemy.

If "B" cells indeed permanently mark the good bacteria for execution - allowing the Crone's condition to cycle for decades until death - the solution to Crone's lies in removing incorrect "antigen" designation within "B" cells.

Until "B" cell rehabilitation is deciphered, Crone's sufferers should calm the immune system down via detoxing, and should chip away at inflammation deposits via enzymes that break inflammation down (these enzymes are describe in chapter 18).

2. Body Heat

One other note on the immune system: it becomes more active when body temperatures rise (fever). One of the reasons Laura took a hot bath each evening was to switch her system to the restful sleep state where the immune system is most active, but the corollary reason was to raise her temperature, even slightly, to further encourage immune cells.

One final note on the immune system …

3. T-Cell Manipulation

One of the difficulties in fighting cancer solely using one's own immune system is that cancer cells appear a natural part of the body to the immune system cells. Cancer is not seen and attacked, the way viruses, bacteria, funguses and parasites are.

The CBD oil, mentioned earlier, helps to make cancer more visible by sticking to the cancer cell walls, making these look somewhat foreign.

And while the CBD tactic helps by illuminating the cancer cells, a reciprocal tactic called Cimetric Antigen Receptor (CAR) T-cells, is in the works that make the immune cells more capable of finding the diseased cells, as follows.

Researchers have found a way to re-configure one's T-Cell gene switches, so that T-Cell "search" receptors more closely pair up with the unique receptors sitting on cancer cell walls. This protocol first harvests T-Cells from the patient, which are then genetically manipulated and allowed to multiply into the billions of cells. These re-configured T-Cells are then infused back into the patient, where they quickly hook up with cancer counterparts, killing the cancer in the same manner immune cells kill all foreigners.

So far this immune system empowerment protocol is used for blood cancers, like leukemia, but it should work for others as well. But just keep in mind, that the core manner for controlling cancer remains not to feed it. Starve the cancer and then send in the troops.

As mentioned earlier, vitamin A is a boost to one's immune cells. Eat plenty of green leafy stuff.

Chapter 13 – Boosting Energy

Common sense dictates that one benefits from as much energy as one can muster during normal times, and that energy grows even more valuable when trying to put cancer back into its box.

"Energy," however, is just a word, and so, this chapter first fleshes out what we mean by "energy" and then elaborates what to do about it in context of the *Self-Healing Protocol.*

What *Is* Energy?

Mankind *barely* understands energy.

Yes, we know how to harness it by burning wood in a fireplace or by creating vast electrical charges in power plants, but that does not mean we understand energy any more than we understand matter.

Einstein advanced our understanding by *imagining* that energy and matter cannot be destroyed, just exchanged, and that the relationship between energy and matter is $E=MC^2$. Still, Albert never said what matter and energy *are*; he just knew how to measure them.

But for sure, it seems certain that when we live, much of this "mysterious" energy resides in our bodies.

And, as stated in an earlier chapter, once the energy ends, the 100-trillion biochemical cell factories pumping away inside of each of us grind to a halt. And we die. So it behooves one to understand the role of energy in one's health, especially if cancer is on the march inside of your body.

But before we talk health, let's talk physics for a brief moment.

Various types of energies employ things called sub-atomic particles to cause their energy "result."

Photons, for example, are *electromagnetic energy* particles that transport light energy. A photon has no weight; it is pure energy. For example, plants capture photons from the sun to fuel photosynthesis.

Electrons are negatively "charged" particles (whatever that really means) pulled toward the positively "charged" protons inside atoms' nuclei.

Somehow electrons can also assemble *en masse* outside of proton influences, such as in the case of lightning bolts, or in the form of *electric energy* moving through our power grids.

PS. I grew up with practicing electrical engineers of the highest rank, the builders of power plants, and none of these gurus could explain any of this. Like Einstein, they knew how to measure electrical phenomenon with equations, but they never could explain the electrical entity itself.

Then there are sub-atomic *nuclear energy* particles called Bosons that hold atoms together. Hey, "Who knew that atoms needed help?"

Sub-atomic *gravitational energy* particles draw discrete bodies together (such as the Earth and the moon), effectively holding the moon and us humans to the Earth. No one has isolated or measured these particles, but we already refer to them as Gravitons. I can only imagine the endless exchange of weightless graviton particles between the Earth and one's feet, likely a gravitational river running all day long!

Phonons are vibrating particles that create a wave effect in air or water. Long-wave length phonons give rise to sound. Shorter wave-length, higher-frequency phonons give rise to heat.

And so, every energy force has its particle facilitator, connecting related entities, and, at every given moment, all of these energy forces and their entire infinitesimal particle exchanges operate according to some grand scheme.

This gigantic interactive energy dynamic proves universally true for stagnant piles of dust, for rocks, for oceans, for the stars, and for our human bodies.

Human bodies? We are surely different than rocks, aren't we?

Life Energy – a force already spoken of in earlier chapters – binds all of these disparate forces together into a coherent living system. Yet as with gravity, we can currently only observe *Life Energy*, and as with gravity, we have not yet isolated its particles.

We gauged *Life Energy*, first in ancient Asian cultures and now in the West, as a network of meridians strung throughout the body. Moreover, one can heighten one's *Life Energy* flow as a boon to one's good health.

In a nutshell, we have observed that where *Life Energy* stands strong, one is near invincible; where *Life Energy* sags weakly, the body loses resolve, and grows ill. And when *Life Energy* leaves the body, the body dies, and returns to dust.

All of this energy stuff, life, gravity, nuclear, light and heat, etc., plays out inside of the biological world.

I have much more to say about *Life Energy* later. But first a look, finally, at its surrogates, the precious mitochondria…

Mitochondria – Biological Energy

Now we'll visit one of the most amazing things I discovered through my recent research: a subspecies called "Mitochondria" living inside of our cells.

As I learned more about this, I would mention the word "Mitochondria" to friends, and it surprised me that they all knew Mitochondria as "the cell's energy power center," drawing comparisons to a Duracell AAA battery.

But that catchphrase proved *all* they knew about the little buggers…

For example, the theory holds that these Mitochondria really exist as a form of bacteria that has lived symbiotically inside our cells... "forever."

"Symbiotically" in this case means that Mitochondria have struck a deal with our cells: they make energy packets used by the cell, and in return, the Mitochondria get to tap into all those juicy nutrients arriving from the cell's outer membrane..

Then I learned that the Mitochondria have their own DNA, meaning that they can reproduce on their own.

I was flabbergasted.

The Mitochondria's DNA stands separate from a cell's big DNA library, which resides inside of the cell's nucleus membrane. Mitochondria have a relatively short DNA strand, as the Mitochondria only do a few things, such as churn molecules to cause energy releases, and divide and multiply to meet the cell's need for energy. (They apparently spin at an amazing 1,000 RPM pace).

The kicker: hundreds up to thousands of these autonomous Mitochondria "things" live inside of every cell of the body ... that's 100 trillion human cells multiplied by thousands of Mitochondria per cell. Gazillions of Mitochondria "agents" live within us – and they are all busy-as-bees making "energy" ... a truly amazing phenomenon for anyone such as myself to contemplate as I thought, "I was I, and only I!" Now I find that I am I ... and a gazillion little buddies.

Note: heart and neuron cells have the most Mitochondria, as these cells are in high gear 24/7. Bone cells might have only a handful.

Apparently these Mitochondria maniacs spin like turbines, day and night, combining phosphates, oxygen, and other molecules, releasing some sort of usable energy packets that propel the endless biochemical activities of the cell.

The energy generated: electrical charges housed in a molecule called ATP, an organic battery that holds an extra electron, which when released powers the chemical processes inside of the cell. I cannot grasp what that actually means, though it is written about in countless medical papers.

But our understanding, as shallow as it is, stops here, as no one can describe how this ethereal energy animates the millions of moving chemical interactions happening within the cell.

Though obviously at the edge of knowledge, by grasping the proliferation of Mitochondria throughout the body, one can nevertheless dimension the vast energy potential of the body. It's energy output is near endless, a perpetual and demanding furnace, burning the nutrients, oxygen and enzymes that keep us alive one moment at a time.

By the way, before we get to the even more-important stuff, I learned that one inherits their Mitochondria from the unfertilized egg supplied by the mother. We refer to Mitochondria DNA as mtDNA and use it in tracking genealogies going all the way back to "Eve."

I wonder, are some people born with better Mitochondria than others? Someone could earn a Ph.D. on this topic alone!

But ponder the bigger questions... What keeps trillions-upon-trillions of Mitochondria spinning? What keeps them working so hard, night and day, cellular division after cellular division - and across an entire human lifetime? And why do they all stop spinning when one dies?

I cannot prove it, but I believe Mitochondria - like from a gruff Newark New Jersey airport cop - get the "keep moving" impulse from the *Life Energy* network pulsating through the body. If the *Life Energy* switch is "on," then all systems are "go." Keep moving! Turn the switch "off" and every Mitochondria light attached to the grid goes out, a permanent power outage.

Despite biology's impressive known and endless unknowns of Mitochondria, I felt that Laura and I ought to help the little buggers out if we could. After all, they remain totally loyal to us on a 24/7 basis, and, more importantly, we apparently (and desperately) need them, as they could simply kill us should they decide to go on strike.

Therapy, Supplements & Double Helix Water

To tend to the wants and desires of these mysterious yet noble Mitochondria, Laura and I decided to use Physical Therapy, Nutritional Supplements, and a special type of water called Double Helix Water to win them over – we offered them the kitchen sink, if you will. I describe each of these protocol elements below.

Physical Therapy - As discussed, Laura met with a Kensiologist on a weekly basis. His job? To determine if any weak energy flows existed in her meridians, and, if so, to take corrective action through manipulation (chiropractic adjustment), stimulation (acupuncture), or through strengthening, (exercising areas of physiological tissue weakness).

As of this writing, Laura attended Kinesiologist evaluation and treatment 30 times. Given the prologue above on energy and health, these weekly (and later bi-monthly) macro-level tune-ups remain essential; we want *all* of the lights on, *all* of the time.

Let's step back. Earlier in the book I mentioned the Thermography heat/cold exam.

They found two points of "trauma" that bookended a specific meridian that runs through Laura's right breast, exactly where the two cancer tumors lined up. The assumption that this "compromised" meridian had not operated properly for an extended period of time implies the following:

Cells along the meridian had long received weak *Life Energy* encouragement from the meridian grid. This, in turn, affected each cell's Mitochondria energy output, which implicitly lowered each cell's ability to fight off outside viruses.

Assuming lower levels of energy prevailed, one must consider that viruses furiously and continuously bombard outer membrane cell walls trying to get in, and that each cell needs to drive millions of internal "protein anti-body and protein crusher molecules" prowling inside to thwart the penetrating invaders. GEEZ!

Each of these operating proteins, though, needs ample energy to fulfill its role, or, as the decidedly politically incorrect saying goes from our baby boomer 1950s childhood: "No ticky, no laundry."

The "low energy" condition similarly affects the immune cells deployed to patrol the breast meridian area; they become sluggish in prosecuting any cancer cells encountered.

The maxim: impeded *Life Energy* leads to illness. The light bulbs may be on, but they glow very dimly. The Kinesiologist worked to get these lights to once again burn brightly.

What else could possibly remain to boost energy levels (besides boosting oxygen, described later)?

<u>The answer: Water</u>"Double Helix Water" proved the most "far-out" finding of my research, but *don't* dismiss it!

Here goes …

Double Helix Water is a physical state of the H^2O water molecule.

The three states of H^2O we know include: ice (solid), water (liquid), and vapor (gas, "steam"), but a fourth state exists…

The fourth state remains an H^2O molecule, but with the atoms packed very tightly together, even more so than when in the ice state (generally as molecules cool, their atomic particles move closer together).

Double Helix Water molecules, however, exist extremely packed together, even when in water of 100-to-200 degrees Fahrenheit.

Rather than through temperature, *Double Helix Water* molecules bind tighter due to extraordinary electrical charges.

OK, so where does this special molecule take us in the discussion of *Life Energy?*

As stated earlier, our bodies are as much as 70 percent water, which amounts to around 100 trillion cells to the "unimaginable" power in water molecules sitting inside all of us, a quantity we cannot possibly fathom.

The *Double Helix Water* molecule exists amongst these, spread evenly throughout the body, with each Double Helix Molecule carrying a super charge of electricity.

I believe that collectively, the *Double Helix Water* charges combine to form the meridian grid within the body, exchanging immense quantities of sub-atomic "charge" particles to cause the effect we call *Life Energy.*

In the laboratory, scientists have found ways to isolate and concentrate the *Double Helix Water* molecules. When put into close proximity, these molecules draw each other closer and – get this – take on the shape of a double-helix DNA strand, forming the spiraling ladder with water molecules rather than genes.

These electrically charged H^2O molecules – found in every glass of water and in every ocean – apparently seek to organize matter across other energy fields (gravity, nuclear, electromagnetic, etc.), into the form of Life's core helix structure.

This did it for me, as I have stood 100 percent sure of *Life Energy's* existence for years having witnessed four births and five deaths, but could never envision a particle exchange framework to hang the concept onto the way all other energy fields function.

Unlike all of the drugs doctors prescribe that are inherently alien to our DNA libraries, water – including the double helix molecules – is inherently natural, fitting in nicely with the overall DNA program. By ingesting concentrated vials of double helix water, one might increase in cellular energy above the norm for, say, a fifty-year old person.

And so, upon understanding the attributes of *Double Helix Water* molecules, I contacted the scientists in California working with *Double Helix Water* and purchased some in order to boost the *Life Energy* current flowing through Laura's body.

The goal: keep all of her cells on their collective toes by keeping the Mitochondria light bulbs burning as brightly as they wanted.

But more, if this all proves true, then *Double Helix Water*, and the helix form it strives for, may explain the backbone of all life on earth (another prospective Ph.D. paper).

Just to finish, a way to understand the Life Energy Grid considers the following: the meridian system already exists in an unfertilized human egg, a circle of energy bands inside the dish-like egg.

Upon fertilization, the egg splits. The split points become the mouth and anus ends of the torso, and the main meridians now run up and down the torso in this vertical manner. As the limbs develop other horizontal meridians branch off to pulsate into these developing peripheral appendages, and so on ...

But one more energy management topic remains... Sleep!

Sleep

Yes, we desire top-of-the-line, clean energy flowing amongst the cells, but we want the cells to rest and repair themselves as well. Therefore, we must understand *sleep* a key element in the *Self-Healing Protocol*.

The nervous system possesses two basic states, *active awake* and *restful sleep* – the middle ground: insomnia and anxiety. Situations can heighten the *active awake* state quite easily to what's called "fight or flight" levels, based on what transpires during the day.

Days where every moment counts, where you find yourself driven, where you encounter threats or trouble, move us further out on the *active awake* spectrum toward "fight or flight."

We also call this "stress."

To cope with stress, one's energy supply "revs" up so that you can ultimately bull yourself through the day. However, this approach does not bode well when trying to kill cancer.

When the system reaches high alert, it focuses energy toward the big fights taking place outside of the body, reducing the energy available for the fights going on inside of the body.

For example, when under stress, the adrenal gland releases a steroid hormone called *Cortisol* to increase sugar and ultimately to suppress the immune system.

When fighting cancer, both of these outcomes are *bad*, and one should shield oneself from as much outside stress as possible to keep energy focused internally (*easier said than done*, but a key factor nonetheless).

Cortisol is important. For a 20-year-old soldier at war, *Cortisol* is a good thing, as it focuses the whole body and mind on the intensity of battle while telling the immune system to "stand down," at least "for now."

But as one ages, the body's ability to deal with "fight or flight" intensity diminishes, yet *Cortisol* release during stress moments stays as constant at age 50 as when just 20 years old.

Ultimately, with age, intense *Cortisol* releases become problematic for many. Indeed, with heart issues, most heart attacks and strokes come within a two-hour window of stress instances, where copious amounts of *Cortisol* remain in the system.

If you have cancer, you must reduce stress-triggers and *Cortisol*-release moments with all of the mental discipline you can muster. Stress, while ill, only serves to further fatigue the body, shut down the immune system, and interrupt healing.

But regardless of how tidily one might arrange one's day during the *active awake* state, the *restful sleep* state must receive an even higher priority.

During the *restful sleep* state, the nervous system switches to "repair" mode, addressing the world *inside* of the body.

At rest, the body channels maximum energy to things such as immune system aggression against foreigners, immune system aggression against cancer cells, DNA repair inside of the cells, orderly cell divisions, and orderly cell deaths, to keep the body's organs and structural tissue on the straight and narrow.

As an example of the role of the *Restful Sleep* state, consider that the body arrests most fevers during *sleep*, when all hands are on the immune system deck.

Overall, each person must optimize their use of energy in both the awake and sleep states toward the fight with cancer.

You achieve optimization by minimizing stress and by getting as much sleep as called for by your body. As you sleep, cancer cells likely die.

In Laura's case, some of the little moves we made included…

- Excluding Laura from inclusion in the "driver pool" on interstate highway trips.

- Laura did *not* attend 40 of our son's all-day travel baseball games, which would exhaust anyone.

- Laura no longer got out of bed at the crack of dawn to let the dogs out (I actually rose to the occasion, surprising even myself).

- On almost a daily basis, Laura took a hot, sea salt bath before bedtime to elevate her body temperature (mentioned earlier), to relax her, to stimulate immune cells and to provide the body with a source of sea salt absorbed through the skin.

- If Laura got worked up over something, I would gently remind her to shut the stress valve off, etc.

- We all tried to treat one another with additional kindness (a special bonus!).

- When Laura returned from Karate on Tuesday and Thursday nights, I always had dinner (salad and sautéed vegetables) ready for her, so as not to cloud the Karate exercises by creating a need or expectation for her to "cook a meal," especially just as her energy reserves hit "empty."

I thought I was doing well ... until Laura complained that I used too much olive oil in sautéing vegetables, and she was right!

Over the course of months calmer *active awake* and *restful sleep* states became the norm. Rather than squandering her enhanced energy levels on the outside world, we channeled these reserves where we wanted them, inside each of Laura's 100 trillion cells.

Energy!

Everything suggested in this chapter is easy to do, so *do* it.

Much of my perspective on stress and survival comes from the book Resilience, by Doctors Southwick and Charney.

Chapter 14 Boosting Oxygen

Understanding Oxygen

As a basic reference point before we get started, our atmosphere currently comprises 21 percent oxygen, with the remainder nitrogen, with a little CO_2 thrown in plus pollutants.

Evidence exists (for instance, from air trapped inside of old amber deposits) that in the past, even in the recent past, the oxygen percentage in the atmosphere may have proven higher, making it easier to breath. Now we breathe faster to gather in the equivalent volume of oxygen.

To start, let's remember that the same oxygen we bring into our bodies via our lungs corrodes almost everything it touches, and it would corrode our cells, too, if that film of anti-oxidants did not coat them.

Good anti-oxidant foods in nature include things such as broccoli, kale and sweet potatoes, but we can find many others, including ...... berries, cherries and lemons (or supplement concentrations of these).

So far so good, simply by eating the "right" foods we can arrange to bring oxygen into the cells without getting hurt in the process.

With the danger of oxygen in mind, we still need to jam endless amounts of oxygen into each cell, so that the cell's mitochondria can combine oxygen with other nutrients to form ATP energy batteries.

The transportation of oxygen to the mitochondria occurs via osmosis, as follows:

1. Oxygen concentrated in the lungs passes through lung membranes into "oxygen empty" red blood cells resulting in "oxygen filled" red blood cells, which the heart pumps forward.

2. At the capillary level, red blood cells come into contact with each body cell's fluid chamber. The high concentration of oxygen in the blood flows into the chamber.

3. From there it enters the cell via special membrane passageways (receptors) not sensitive to the corrosive nature of oxygen.

4. Finally, the oxygen molecules are moved to the cell's mitochondria sub-chamber to oxidize food nutrients.

Conversely, once nutrients are oxidized (burned) and CO_2 is generated, the CO_2 gas escapes from the cell and returns to the lung for exhalation using the same osmosis dynamics in reverse.

What can we do to help?

Oxygen Enhancement

We know that people with cancer have lower metabolized oxygen levels circulating in their blood streams as compared to others in the general population.

And remember, both viruses and cancer cells thrive in low oxygen environments, so besides detoxing to elevate "oxygen friendliness", oxygen "volume" boosting remains a must, but where to start?

Clumping – Research shows that as we age, our red blood cells start to clump while moving through the system. As an illustration, forty cells clumped together cannot grab and deliver the same amount of oxygen as 40 autonomous cells, because autonomous cell walls remain completely exposed at all turns, allowing them to pick up a maximum amount of oxygen from the lungs and deliver that maximum to the 100 trillion cells "breathing" throughout the body.

The tiny capillaries, which bring blood down to the cellular level, are so small that red blood cells need to pass through in single file. Clumped blood never enters the capillaries; it simply circulates around the big veins and arteries never reaching the cells to deliver nutrients and oxygen.

With this as the big picture, it is safe to say that we don't like "clumping"! Before suggesting a solution to clumping, let's first dimension the oxygen transport infrastructure in the body.

I cannot begin to estimate how many oxygen atoms we take in with every breath we breathe, so again, I will use my pretend number "gazillions."

On average we breathe 17,000 times a day, and so you can imagine the elegance of the system, one that delivers an almost infinite stream of oxygen atoms to all of our 100 trillion cells on a continual basis.

Any impediment to this Goliath delivery mechanism has to be bad, very bad. Each one percent in oxygen deficiency affects every cell in the body by one percent, and deeper deficiencies ultimately cause "tipping-point" enfeeblement among the cells, a recipe for viral intensity, cancer development, and tumor growth.

As said, "We don't like clumping."

It chokes off oxygen.

Laura and I use light photons to un-clump the blood as follows:

Think about photons. When the sun comes out, flowers open, and turn toward that light source. The sun's photons infuse continuous energy into every cell in the plant.

Not only does this photon bombardment cause photosynthesis (chemical stuff), it also causes THE ENTIRE PLANT TO MOVE!

We *like* photons.

And I do mean "we," as in "us," the humans. But liking photons means more than merely enjoying a walk in the sun. Liking photons means that human cells *like* photons just the way plant cells do. Though we can't gather photons in the manner of plants (plants have leaves), our skin *does* gather photons to make things like Vitamin D – *our* version of photosynthesis.

Deeper human cells, though, do not enjoy exposure to the sun, but if they did, they would soak up the photon energy, supplementing energy that the tiny Mitochondria chemically produce down in the trenches.

Now let's look at oxygen and photons in context of "clumping" red blood cells.

As a start, red blood cells contain no nucleus. Red blood cells exist merely as "temporary" quasi-cells, shot out from the bone marrow to lug nutrients and oxygen around, programmed to die within 30-to-60 days.

But as one ages, the new red blood cells, born day-in and day-out, begin emerging in a weakened state, containing less and less energy due to the erosion of genetic data caused by over-extended stem cell divisions within the bone marrow. So they clump together in a type of old-age desperation.

Here it comes...

Photon Devices

If one blasts red blood cells in older people with photons, the red clusters un-clump! (So I read)

By exposing red blood cells to a huge blast of natural photon energy, like every other cell living under the sun, the red cells know how to metabolize the incoming photon energy packets. This boost causes the tired cells to kick into gear, at least for a while, allowing the to un-clump.

A company in Canada, called *VieLight*, sells such a photon delivery system. One attaches a small infrared light clip into one's nostril, which blasts photons for 25 minutes into the nasal cavity.

Other than the tongue, the nasal cavity experiences the most concentrated amount of blood passing through a contained area per second. In 25 minutes, all the blood in the body passes through the nasal cavity, and the infrared light beam gives each red blood cell a photon boost.

Once boosted, the red cells de-clump from each other. Soon these red cells flow through the lungs autonomously and deliver increased oxygen throughout the body - the way red blood cells do within a healthy, young 16-year-old's system.

By the next day the red cells have used up their temporary photon boost and they begin clumping again, so you plug the light back into your nose, read a book, and un-clump a few billion red blood cells all over again.

The cancer cells will hate the whole experience.

By the way, photon "guns" and "braces" are available to "shoot" photons into, say, a sprained ankle. Injuries heal twice as fast with photon boosting. I have used this approach on four occasions within my family. That is why I knew that every cell simply LOVES protons!

Can you dig it?

Ok, what else?

Resveratrol

A final oxygen enhancement tactic involves opening up the blood vessels themselves.

Like all parts of the body, vessel cells, too, "lose altitude" as we age, and it behooves one to open them up a bit to get the blood moving freely and to deliver more oxygen faster.

How does one do this?

Well ... an organic molecule called "Resveratrol" does just this. Resveratrol relaxes vessels, causing greater elasticity throughout vessel membranes, allowing them to expand and contract with less resistance during each and every heartbeat. Blood moves fluidly, as it wants to.

Resveratrol is extracted from red grape skins, and marketed in pill form. Red grape wine is known to reduce heart disease (the so-called "French wine effect") due to the resveratrol in the red wine, which loosens up the system, reducing stress on the heart. So take Resveratrol.

And speaking of blood vessel walls, don't forget about glycation, mentioned earlier, where sugar binds with anti-aging proteins to further harden vascular channels.

Now, to tie everything said in this chapter together, consider this fact as well: with her energy system tuned up to the hilt, Laura does some form of exercise daily, be it Karate, jogging, or the gym … which all moves lots of oxygen, lots of energy. I only gave this one paragraph, but Laura implemented this SIX DAYS A WEEK!

Before moving beyond oxygen please consider the following:

An Alternative Cancer Theory Involving Oxygen

Since 1931, when a Dr. Warburg won a noble prize on the subject, some believe that cancer is nothing more than a normal cell whose oxygen levels have fallen to the point where the mitochondria have given up, causing the cell to switch over to pure anaerobic fermentation.

Once in this state cells cut off communication with the body, ceasing to "hear" the *apoptosis* signals to die, etc. In this isolated state the cells simply devour glucose and divide so long as they are fed.

Toxins, smoking, poor circulation, clumping etc. are just some of the reasons an adequate oxygen supply no longer reaches the cells.

Another observation cited by advocates of this theory points to higher fermentation burn rates of aggressive cancers as compared to slow growing cancer. High fermentation rates require a robust supply of sugar in the blood due to diet.

Another complementary observation indicates that cancer cells are poisoned by oxygen, once they no longer burn oxygen in a controlled setting; hence cancer cells only experience the destructive side of oxygen.

Theories aside: get your oxygen going... just to be sure.

PART VI
INFILTRATING CANCER

Chapter 15 – Send in The Trojan Horses

If you follow sports, you will embrace the following: A good defense is as important as a good offense. All of this proper eating, cleanliness, immune system enhancement, oxygen boosting and meridian energizing tactics make up your offensive attack, whereas defense means messing with your opponent to drive them well out of their comfort zone.

A resourceful friend of mine advised me to have Laura ingest baking soda, as cancer hates pro-oxygen alkaline baking soda. Consuming actual baking soda seemed a very direct approach, much more aggressive than just eating alkaline causing foods. So I looked into it. And thus the "Trojan Horse" surfaced.

Rather than flood the blood system with backing soda that would, at best, make cancer cells somewhat uncomfortable, we found a way to trick the cancer cells into devouring large amounts of baking soda imbedded in something cancer craves, a technique I referred to in the book's Introduction as *infiltration*.

With this approach, one could "kick back" and let the cancer tumors "freak out" over their bad decision to let a wooden horse in. Two initial Trojan Horse techniques surfaced, but others followed over time:

Honey & Baking Soda

Remember how much cancer loves sugar? How it gobbles it up during PETScans? Well the following approach infuses baking soda inside of honey sugar and feeds the "totally" contaminated honey to the ravenous cancer cells.

I like it!

The enemy "turncoat" cancer cells greedily ingest the honey's sugar and, in doing so, the intolerable amounts of backing soda hidden within stick to them like a cancer-fighting glue. The preparation for the honey/baking soda mixture follows...

Combine half a cup of honey and half a cup of baking soda in a glass.

Place glass in a stovetop pan with heated water and stir for 8 minutes.

Ingest a tablespoon each day.

Hemp Oil & Frankincense Oil

This second Trojan Horse presents a similar approach: Frankincense, an essential oil, confuses cancer cells over whether to divide or not, as the frankincense somehow inhibits the division trigger.

Note: By "essential" medical people mean that the body cannot make the compound in question internally, and hence, if you want the compound, it is "essential" to ingest it from outside the body.

To get the "traitorous" cancer cells to ingest the Frankincense, the Frankincense is mixed into "CBD" hemp oil by a Colorado firm called "Bluebird".

CBD oil is gleaned from hemp plants, which we once used to make rope. CBD molecules happen to have receptors that match up with cancer cell receptors, so that by ingesting hemp oil, one effectively coats the cancer tumor with hemp gook, which itself, like an anti-body, attracts immune cells.

By mixing in some frankincense with the hemp oil, you have delivered a double blow to the tumor.

The CBD oil first serves as an anti-body beacon to lure immune cells, and second, through osmosis, the tumor absorbs the unwanted frankincense right into its gut.

It's a two-for-one deal!

Screw 'em!

Intravenous Vitamin "C" Considered

Some alternative-therapy practitioners, including the aforementioned Mexican doctor, advocate intravenous injection of megadoses of vitamin C.

The direct injection of the vitamin prevents the digestive tract from compromising the C molecule. Proponents claim that the body converts concentrated C into substances that affect the anaerobic mechanism these rogue cells depend upon.

The derived compound contains H2O2 (hydrogen peroxide), which, in turn, floods cancer cells with unwanted oxygen. Due to the requirement to have an IV installed, we did not look further into this therapy, but hope that "science" can get closer to it, as it seems a plausible construct.

Other advocates suggest bypassing the mega C step, and simply ingesting low dosages of hydrogen peroxide in distilled water. We also passed on this, for now, as I feared using an incorrect dosage.

Ok, everything described so far took place over the first ninety days of the protocol. There was more to come.

PART VII
GRIT AND GRACE

Chapter 16 – Month 3 Breakthrough

The 90-day Photograph

Almost 90 days passed since we learned of the cancer. Time for another trip to New York City to re-measure Laura's tumors using the 3-D Sonogram, time to determine if anything we were doing or thinking works.

It started good and ended, shall we say … well, you'll see…

We set our meeting with the doctor for 2:30 pm, as inspired planning allowed time for lunch in Manhattan. So we enjoyed lunch with *Toni and Vinnie*, our best NYC friends ever. At lunch, spirits remained high, based simply upon Laura's "look" and energy, and simply, at our pleasure in sitting with people of our inner circle … especially at lunch … on Manhattan's Columbus Circle.

We left the restaurant confident, never losing our core conviction that things were working; yet as we walked the hot midtown NYC streets on the way to the doctor's office, each NYC block became heavier and hotter!

The doctor's office felt extremely warm, just having crossed midtown in the blazing sun… so we "sweated," waiting our turn to receive the verdict.

Finally, the receptionist gives us "the sign" and brings us to one of the examination rooms. The good Doctor (and I *mean* it) walks in and instantly engages us as if we had just seen each other earlier that day.

Today he is all business, as he, too, wants to see what had transpired across recent time. He spots the titanium markers sitting inside of the right breast and looks for the tumors. We follow the analysis on the screen monitor.

The smaller one is no longer visible, the Doctor pronounces calmly. A half-a-minute later, he proclaims *the bigger tumor has shrunken by half.*

That's it?

After all of those months, days, and hours, it took but a mere minute or two to determine that "We were good"?

Witnessing the evidence on the video screens with my own two eyes, I next remember paying the $800 bill and leaving.

During it all, Laura and I show no sign of joy whatsoever. We had "steeled" ourselves not to react to news, good *or* bad.

Walking up the street, Laura asks, "*Shouldn't we be happy?*"

I answer, "*We are.*"

Our next 3D Sonogram appointment would take place 150 days out.

Next Steps and Daily Life

Do you remember how I found my first wife chain-smoking cigarettes, saying that her fight days were over? Well, the *Self-Healing Protocol* is a long-range strategy, and the protocol absolutely warrants flexibility to cultivate stamina. And so, driving out of Manhattan, to finally celebrate, I pull the car over and get Laura a slice of pizza.

But after that, it was "back to basics" protocol-wise, yet not at the intensity maintained during the first 90 days. Leading up to the 3D Ultrasound check-up, Laura, over a stretch of 21 days, went "super extreme" in consuming a zero-sugar- and-fat diet while eating only alkaline vegetables for a truly inspiring run of discipline.

As a result, the good news regarding tumor shrinkage meant this: *Laura's whole body had taken up the offensive... and it was winning.*

So one should keep it up, right?

Yes, but you run the 100-yard dash differently than the NYC Marathon. So use the momentum of the good results as the fuel source for a long run, right? Let's not burn willpower up by forcing endless 100-yard sprints...

The first 90 days proved special in other ways as well. For one, they addressed the excess triglycerides and toxins sitting inside Laura's 100 trillion cells and had "shown them the door" with conviction.

Laura, now at her "young woman's" weight, had met these essential milestones.

On day 90, Laura's nourishment transpired solely by what she ate *that day* and not by long-forgotten substances, buried inside her body for decades. The flow of glucose through her body was even, and moderated to the level needed by healthy cells.

There were no gushing sugar spikes coming in to relieve the cancer, (though later I would uncover more insight into subtle sugar spikes and diabetic conditions – described at the end of the book). This meant that we could alter the protocol to some degree, something that Holistic Doctor also recommended.

Laura started by eating fish and chicken every other day while still depriving the ever-shrinking cancer colonies. Watching Laura go off to karate each day, I felt better that we had reintroduced some low-fat, semi-alkaline sources of protein. For the next 150 days, Laura continued to consume fish or chicken every other day.

Chapter 17 – Month 8, Almost There

The Plan

At the end of October, the schedule called for us to return to NYC to have a third 3D sonogram image compiled of her large tumor (you'll recall that the small tumor had already disappeared by the time of the second sonogram five months earlier).

We felt pretty confident that the results would prove good, as Laura had stuck to the already-effective *Self-Healing Protocol* all along. But more so, throughout this second four-month tenure, with her body clear of toxins and triglyceride reserves and her immune system *empowered*, she had truly *deprived* and persistently *infiltrated* the cancer.

By September, seven months in, Laura had settled into her new weight, her ideal 113 pounds – the same as in her twenties. She looked and felt great, with her cells living in an environment of no toxins, plenty of oxygen, vigorous immune responses, reduced microbe activity, passive cancer remnants, no sugar, caffeine, or alcohol-like stimulants and a steady flow of alkaline-tilting nutrients.

Laura's system hummed. And so, like a closing pitcher in Major League Baseball, it came time to *really* pour it on.

By this I mean bringing her life energy up to a higher plane by introducing the Double Helix Water and the CoQ10 supplements, already described, to deliver the "final blows" to end the war, at least for now.

The Double Helix Water would heighten electrical energy inside of every cell in the body, spurring each cell's mitochondria to gear up, as the CoQ10 fed the mitochondria the enzyme they needed to work at this elevated level.

We set another goal for October, "to live a little," to get fresh psychological momentum transitioning into the upcoming *Living Wisely* phase of the protocol (though this would backfire should the late October test bring bad news).

I called this "The October Offensive." But before launching the troops, so to speak, first we took stock in where we stood.

The Kinseologist

The Kinseologist found no remaining issues in Laura's energy-balancing status.

The Biological Dentist

The Biological Dentist retested Laura for toxins (pesticides, heavy metals, funguses, preservatives, tooth and gut microbe excretions, etc.), and found no remaining levels.

As we never removed her root canal tooth, he captured an electronic image of possible microbe toxins emanating from the tooth, and made a special water vial of this image for Laura to take in October.

The Holistic Doctor

The Holistic Doctor took a blood test to check Laura's levels. Almost every category had become optimal. For example, Laura's Triglycerides now ran just 43 rather than 130. Her vitamin levels placed well within range, and her thyroid numbers good, though her white blood count was slightly elevated.

A Special Blood Test

Months earlier, during one of my research nights, I stumbled upon the *Serum TK* blood test (no longer available) that tests for the degree of cell division in the body. As some cells die and others divide (the programmed Apoptosis and Mitosis routines previously described), the process leaves a certain bi-product serum behind in the blood stream. If cancer is on the rise, with millions of cells abnormally dividing, this serum level rises at a measurable rate.

I purchased two test packages on-line.

We would get a baseline test of Laura's serum level now, in October of 2014, using the first test pack to benchmark cell division as it currently stood, and planned to measure activity later on, say, in six months' time, using the second test pack. After killing off the visible cancer we would need a "trust and verify" scheme… and this was to be part of it (a second, similar test surfaced later as well).

The results of the Serum TK test indicated that cancer activity still existed somewhere in Laura's system. But we now had a specific serum level to use going forward to gauge positive or negative cell division momentum.

Double Helix Water, Revisited

With all of these preparations in hand, I called the Double Helix Water people again.

I mentioned earlier that I had contacted their California office to discuss the concept and the history of this hard-to-imagine find. Since that initial call, I had read the book published by Doctors Gann and Lo, the two scientists behind it all. I called Jon, the fellow with whom I had spoken previously. I again found him communicative, able to discuss matters at any level, theoretical, testing, protocol, etc.

I asked about the relative concentration of Double Helix water molecules in regular water, as compared to the vials of water they would send me.

Each vial would contain one million more Double Helix molecules than tap or seawater. These would be distributed throughout the body in a pro rata manner across 100 trillion cells (remember, the body is 70 percent water).

Because of the number of cells (100 trillion), the protocol for breast cancer meant ingesting seven vials of Double Helix water each day. This would raise the standing electrical charge in each cell to an optimal level, double the charge a typical older person carries due to a dwindling "power supply."

The elevated charge, spread and pulsated via the meridian system, would push every cell to operate at its 18-year-old potential. The mitochondria would spin for all they were worth, and the CoQ10 would provision the mitochondria to operate comfortably at this aggressive pace.

Presumably, cells would no longer tolerate viruses, and immune cells would "take no prisoners" in their pursuit of foreign (antigen) invaders.

I ordered a whole bunch of vials, and we purchased some CoQ10 from a health food store.

An American Indian Remedy

For centuries, a famous "tea" consisting of forest matter used by American Indians from the Toronto area, has earned a reputation for thwarting cancer.

I do not know why so many believe it works, but so many sources had mentioned this tea over the past months that I decided to throw it into the mix now, in October 2014, for good measure.

We bought some at a health food store and Laura drank it until we ran out.

Let's Roll

OK, our October plan is in place, what else? Oh yeah… "Live a little."

Laura wears her "New York Giants Fan" heart on her sleeve, with Eli Manning the entire NY Giant franchise in her eyes. For years, I have watched Laura scream bloody murder at Eli on national television should he commit the slightest miscue.

Thankfully, the attack does not fall solely upon Eli. For instance, Laura's scathing criticism buried Eli's big brother Peyton throughout the 2014 Super Bowl, a worse attack from Laura than Peyton experienced from that West Coast team, whoever *they* were (the Seahawks, of course).

Young Eli, though, does gain relief from criticism whenever Laura attacks the refs … such as when the opposition tackled Eli in the end zone, gaining two points for the deed *and* possession of the ball (it's called a "safety"). Laura followed this decision against the Giants with accusations of cash exchanges and referee corruption taking place right on national TV, with Laura, of course, the only person in America to see through it all.

Then the play where an opposition wide receiver circled back and executed the old Statue of Liberty "handoff" from his own quarterback, advancing 20 yards. Laura went ballistic, screaming *"Where the hell are the refs, doesn't anyone else see this; they just stole their own ball!"*

My favorite: the time Eli threw a bunch of interceptions against Green Bay. From several rooms away, I heard her screaming *"Eli, you know what you are? You're (expletive deleted)."* I came running in to learn the cause of the commotion and Laura blurted out *"Eli keeps throwing the ball to the guys in the green outfits..."*

Well, you get the point... "Giants or death", though I prefer "live free or die".

On Saturday night, October 6th, at 11 pm, the dam broke, and I decided to buy good seats on *Stubhub* for Laura, myself, and our son Joseph, for the very next day's Sunday, October 7th game against the Atlanta Falcons.

The game would start at 1 pm at MetLife Stadium in Rutherford, N.J. It would mean six hours of round-trip driving time, which violated the "no stress" protocol, but so what! Laura did not plan on eating those stadium hot dogs, washing them down with the $12 beers, so we left early, went to a local store, and bought her special grub to bring into the stadium.

The George Washington Bridge, of course, provided two automobile accidents, one on the upper level and one on the lower. We sat in the snarled traffic, and Laura's blood began to boil. She agreed to calm down. No need to produce Cortisol over a slight delay in the plan.

It was Laura's first time in the stands at an NFL game. The sun glowed brightly producing a perfect 65 degrees Fahrenheit, and the Giants had just scored as we entered the stadium, late by 20 minutes.

Atlanta scored as we found our seats. Eli next threw a few bad passes, and Atlanta scored twice more. Laura sat devastated going into halftime.

In the second half Eli finally found his game, pounding away, finding Cruz and Beckham. Laura had her chance to scream in unison with the thousands of Giants fans and exchange multiple high-fives, and depart with a 30-to-20 Giant comeback victory notched on her belt.

Thank you, Eli, *thank* you.

Crossing back over the George Washington Bridge, we passed Columbia Presbyterian Hospital and I recalled that troubling episode months earlier and reflected upon how far Laura had come in a relatively small number of months with her *own* second-half comeback.

The Third 3D Sonogram

A few weeks later we were back in New York to see Doctor Bard and get a third 3D sonogram measurement of the remaining tumor. The results were good, as the tumor had flattened out. It was the same length, but it had lost most of its depth and width.

On this visit Doctor Bard prescribed his own supplements, a strong concoction of Primrose-based anti-oxidants, some CoQ10, and something to temper the dense breast tissue situation, which he explained resulted in four times the occurrence of breast cancer (more on dense breast tissue later).

We left in good spirits.

Chapter 18 – Month 12, No Tumors

It's Been a Year...

Finally, in February of 2015, Laura's one-year check-up date arrived.

The last tumor measurement took place in October 2014, four months prior. Back then, no sign of the smaller tumor appeared, but the shrunken larger tumor remained visible. Now, after another 120 days, we would find out if the gods continued to smile upon us.

Laura stayed on track during those 120 days... well, sort of. First during Thanksgiving, and then during Christmas and New Year's, various food liberties transpired on multiple occasions.

Overall, though, 80 percent of the protocol stayed intact. Laura took her supplements, continued her exercise, and her food consumption never included sugar, carbohydrate, or acidic red meat. Yes, a glass of red wine had become standard fare with dinner, with chicken and fish almost daily.

Still, Laura worried that she had let up on the gas pedal. I reminded her that a) she still followed the protocol at the 80 percent level and b) that all of the detoxification benefits accrued during the first six months of the protocol remained in place. Her acidic toxins were gone.

She noted that from a weight of 113 pounds for almost a year, the January 10th scale suddenly read "118." (Quietly, I gulped – wrong direction!)

The drive into Manhattan from our Connecticut residence typically takes two-and-a-half hours, but anything can happen once you get near the city.

To avoid unknown delays, we decided to drive halfway to the city, stopping in Brewster, New York, to park the car and take the Metro North commuter train into Grand Central Terminal on 42nd street.

Arriving in the city at 11:45 am, we head through the frigid streets, making our way to 44th street and a favorite New York destination, the Greek seafood restaurant Kellari Taverna.

While enjoying all of the restaurant's great energy and food, I ask Laura if she feels nervous about her doctor's appointment. Her answer: *There's nothing that can be done now, so why worry?*

We had grown measured and even stoic over the course of the year.

The doctor, happy to see us, appears generally optimistic, although before getting started he cautions: *These things can get better, but they can slip backward, too. Let's take a look...*

Laura goes off with a physician's assistant for a mammogram. Next, we sit in the waiting room until asked into the doctor's office.

Well, I have good news. The mammogram does not show any tumors. The two titanium markers are visible, but no sign of tumors. Let's go into the examination room and try the sonogram.

The doctor examines both breasts and the lymph nodes in each armpit, saying that all of the nodes are clear. Then he goes back to the right breast.

I still see something where the large tumor was... it may be the last remnant of the tumor, or it may be scar tissue, but at least we have a picture of it for future reference.

I can also tell you that the breast density found on previous visits has been reduced. Looking us in the eye, he notes: *Dense breast tissue is a marker for development of new outbreaks, so the improvement is very encouraging.*

Please recall that four months ago Dr. Bard had prescribed his own brand of anti-oxidants and vascular support supplements designed to address both anti-oxidant goals and the breast density issue.

And, with a smile, he says: *You two should go home and not worry about this for six months. Come back in the summer and we'll take another look.*

Privately, "the Irish" side of me was going to worry "a wee bit" longer!

Then he turned to me and asks: *What about you? I see you haven't come in for a prostate exam. You should be tested every six months.* (The 3D sonogram system is used for prostate examinations as well). I agree to sign up for an exam when we return in the summer.

We hop a cab to Grand Central Station and head home. While on the train, I send a text out to our four children, telling them the good news.

Now what?

Driving home from the Brewster train station, Laura brought the subject up, saying: *The doctor seemed a little cryptic…*

I weighed in: *He reported as clearly as possible. The mammogram showed no tumors and we'ld look at the tumor sites again in six months' time to check the residue tissue.*

Then can I cut back on taking some of these pills, she mused?

I don't know, I replied. *Everything you take has a clear purpose. Let's just get through this week and we can regroup next week.*

By "getting through this week," I referred to my own immediate travel plans and Laura's second-tier black belt test, coming up in a few days' time.

The next day I take off on a three-day side trip to New Orleans with my oldest daughter; she to do research for her undergraduate thesis, and me, to tag along.

I wished for Laura to make the Louisiana trip as well, but she needed to stay home to train and rest in preparation for her second-degree black belt test that coming Sunday.

I had mixed feelings about the black belt event only because it constitutes a big deal, physically. One fights 10 opponents for one minute each, with the karate master demanding "I want to see you fight!"

In "protocol-think," this means huge amounts of Cortisol created by the body in an ultimate "fight or flight" scenario.

And I worried not just about those 10 minutes of constant battle… Leading up to fight day, Laura would hone her fighting chops as well as her cardiovascular stamina with daily prep sessions. To me, this meant even more Cortisol, more lactic acid, and more inflammation.

But still, I knew I had a fighter on my hands, and fighting is what a fighter does.

As I leave for Louisiana, Laura agrees to take the hot baths each night so that her body can switch off the combat hormones and induce the sleep and rest hormones.

We touch base each day.

When I return from Louisiana on Saturday evening, Laura appears tired, but ready for her Sunday promotion test the next morning.

At the "dojo" (Japanese karate centers are called dojos), I recognize many senior black belt veterans from previous years who had traveled from different locations across America to attend, with many 5th-degree black belt masters in attendance, both male and female. That day, Laura would fight 10 of them.

Other black belts up for promotion fight before her, and one fellow gets hurt, tearing his ACL. It is tough, grim business, and I cringe watching each punch or kick landed.

Then comes Laura's good friend Audrey's turn. One by one, the international master calls 10 challengers up, and Audrey starts to hammer away.

With her first opponent, Audrey's right hand gets cut. Next, during her spar with the second challenger, her left knuckle is cut. As Audrey landed punches, blood stains the white smocks (called ghis in Japanese) of each opponent. After five challengers, a woman runs out to place bandages on Audrey's hands, but Kaicho, the master, calls her off, as this would allow Audrey to catch her breath.

It doesn't matter. Fight!

Finally, it ends. I turn to Audrey's husband and joke, *Well, she bloodied every one of them.*

His response: *Too bad it's her blood.*

Laura stands up, wanting to fight next.

Laura does not hold back. High kicks and punching flourishes continued through the first four fights, until she takes a bad kick to her left leg and staggers. She gets kicked there again by the next fighter and the master yells to keep fighters from going after that leg, while still demanding that the fight continues with full force.

A veteran, Laura keeps her energy source as aerobic, pacing herself, relaxing even while in combat to keep her breathing at its optimum level.

But by fighter number eight, her aerobic stamina wanes. Her willpower triggers the painful anaerobic creation of energy lasting until the finish.

It goes on and on, and finally it ends.

Almost!

The master tells Laura to do 25 knuckle push-ups. At 25, the master calls for 10 more, then 10 more, and then 10 more.

Standing up, Laura next has to kick 10 tennis balls hanging from the ceiling above her head. If she misses one, the count starts over. She gets five and misses Number 6. At some point she reaches 10, five kicked with her right leg and five with her injured left leg.

Next, the master gives Laura a broomstick, which she holds with both hands. While holding it, she must jump over the broomstick so that it ends up behind her, and then jump back to bring the broomstick forward again.

She must complete this task 10 times, while the dojo counts in Japanese.

If she stumbles, the count began anew. Laura stumbles more than once, until her vast power of the mind takes over and she cleanly jumps back-and-forth 10 times.

"*Enough!*" the master proclaims.

The room applauds as Laura, drenched in perspiration, sits down next to Audrey.

Chapter 19 – Digging Deeper

The next phase is upon us

"Next week" comes quickly, time to regroup and talk about the protocol going forward.

Laura and I chat first about food. Laura says she does not want to change her diet. She now loves kale and beets for instance, and finds red meat revolting. When we visit a steakhouse, Laura will flip directly to the chicken and fish options on the menu.

Yes, Laura takes a lot of supplements, well-targeted supplements, and if you crush all of the pills, it only comes to a small pile of dust ingested, along with the three-to-four quarts of food and liquid she consumes each day.

Regardless of these "reasonable" proportions, Laura's tolerance for pill taking is sinking fast.

Rather than expecting to reduce her supplements, secretly I had uncovered additional supplements that I itched to pitch to Laura...

Enzymes

For example, we could now consider the topic of enzymes. Mentioned earlier, I held off on this topic throughout the whole year of the protocol, other than adding CoQ10, which, technically, constitutes a co-enzyme, used by the mitochondria to convert incoming nutrients into energy.

In general, enzymes are internally created chemicals made by the body that cause other chemical reactions to take place. Enzymes are catalysts, but they need other players such as co-enzymes to work their magic.

Enzymes operate down in the chemical trenches of one's bodily fluids, causing *chemical byproducts*, not to be confused with hormones, chemical triggers operating at a higher level, directing *cellular behavior*.

The body creates and deploys thousands of enzymes to cause a host of chemical-transposing results, such as breaking down food in the intestines. One might consider taking "Digestive Enzymes," for example, as a supplement.

Another example: When you get hurt, inflammation (think "sticky goo") takes place, causing pain so that the body stays quiet while healing steps take place.

Enzymes eventually move in to corrode the inflammation, to flush it out of the system, relieving pain.

OK, so different centers of the body create thousands of enzyme components, addressing thousands of biological objectives. One objective focuses on reducing breast fibrosis via scar tissue elimination enzymes, as follows:

First an aside … for the purposes of fighting cancer, some advocate that certain enzyme supplements can "spur on" the immune system and that other enzymes can "corrode" the walls of cancer cells. I could find nothing to substantiate these claims, so I passed on these, but my ears remain open.

Scar tissue and breast density

And now my practical proposition regarding enzymes and breast cancer.

I don't know how many times I heard and read that women with "dense" breast tissue are four (4) times as likely to get breast cancer than woman without dense breast tissue.

Yet no one, and no writing I could find, suggested a) why dense breast tissue occurred (fibrosis) in the first place, or b) why dense tissue would lead to four (4) times the occurrence of breast cancer for these women.

Now that Laura and I had destroyed the tumors, I pondered this four-times-as-likely topic, figuring that if not confronted, any propensity for fresh cancer outbreaks would be unchecked, allowing cancer to re-propagate.

So I asked myself: *What the heck do they mean by 'dense breast tissue' and why could this condition lead to disease?*

Susan G Komen, on her Breast Cancer website, explains:

Breast density is not a measure of how the breasts feel, but rather how the breasts look on a mammogram. High breast density means there is a greater amount of breast connective tissue (fibrosis) as compared to fat. Low breast density means there is a greater amount of fat as compared to breast and connective tissue.

OK, get ready to contemplate the following idea. If correct, breast cancer sufferers and all aging persons will sing "halleluiah"!

<u>What is scar tissue?</u>

Have you ever thought of this?

Again, what is scar tissue? You have heard about it all of your life!

First, scar tissue is not alive. It is a string of proteins that certain guardian cells create whenever the body suffers damage. Ejected protein strings from the guardians bind damaged tissue together until it heals.

Scar tissue is a bunch of chemical strings that envelope damaged cells and leftover stocks of inflammation gook. All of this stuff is DEAD!

wiseGEEK explained scaring as follows:

Internal scar tissue can be formed by various causes including repetitive usage. The healing process will begin by forming fibrosis tissue around the injury, effectively forming a web that protects it from further harm.

During this stage the injured cells turn into adhesions, which are basically dead cells. The fibrosis tissue, along with a body chemical known as collagen, then begins working to repair the damaged area with new cells. As the area heals, the adhesions that were present will develop into permanent scar tissue.

Fundamentally, we should not refer to it as scar "tissue" as tissue implies living cells fed by blood and lymph networks. Scars are simply dead organic masses that often stay with you until you die.

Personally, I have all kinds of scare tissue buried in my body due to injury and age, so I get it. And it hurts!

So I looked into both "stringy scar tissue" and the "inflammatory goo" which the body's Neutrophil immune cells mindlessly park around traumatized tissues.

What I found: the body, apparently, makes enzymes that rid these necessary evils once they have done their job.

Two interesting enzymes called "Wobenzyme-N" and SEFFAFLAZYME surfaced. They apparently corrode inflammatory goo and scar tissue itself. Research in the 1990s by a Doctor Lee isolated these enzymes.

We apparently create anti-inflammatory/anti-scarring enzymes in large quantities only up until the age of 27; and perhaps that explains why younger people can come back from injury much faster and better than older people. The construct of these "injury mop up" enzymes is as follows:

Both young and old bodies create scar "tissue" to mend injured tissue. With younger bodies, scarring represents a temporary step towards full rehabilitation of the damaged tissue. After the string-like scar protein has done its job – holding the damaged area together – the scar-busting enzymes come in and corrode the scar fibers away so that primary tissue can fill in where scar matter once resided.

Because older people (past age 27) have reduced supplies of these enzymes, they tend to accumulate scar proteins as the years go by, never purging them, and they learn to live with the chronic inflammation that scarring represents.

The Big Idea (Finally)

My proposition: fibrosis of the breast is nothing more than scar fibers resulting from the monthly wear-and-tear of the menstrual cycle.

As breast cells divide and die each month, bits of fibrosis result, building up over decades.

The fibrosis scar and inflammation goo clogs everything up, making the breast tissue "dense".

As a result of the clutter, some women have reduced blood/ lymph support to combat viruses and budding cancer colonies incubating amongst the good fat cells suffocating within the breast.

So if breast density claims nothing more than string-like scare fibers and inflammatory goo, would the Wobenzyme-N and SEFFAFLAZYME enzymes help to ameliorate the "density" condition?

The idea for adding Wobenzyme-N and SEFFALAZYME as supplements is three-fold. First, they will reverse some of the aging effects of scar tissue throughout the body caused by a lifetime of traumatic *skeletal* injuries.

Second, *micro* scar tissue and chronic inflammatory deposits accumulated due to wear and tear in the organs can also be reduced systemically (body-wide), providing greater vascular support to these work horse organs.

Third, In the case of dense breast conditions, the enzyme might corrode some of the fibrosis and inflammatory deposits, restoring vascular support – provisioning nutrients, oxygen and immune cells – that will keep breast cells healthier going forward.

This might be too good to be true, but if nature has created a complex enzyme to perfectly address scar tissue and inflammation, then I would trust this natural compound.

Note: I personally tried Wobenzyme first as a test case. A week into it I drove one college daughter three hours to school on a Saturday, and a second daughter six hours to school the next day, Sunday. Pulling up to the driveway at the end of the Sunday marathon, I feared stepping out of the car. In recent years, car time meant pain time. Yet I stood up with minimal stiffness.

A week later, I realized that I was sleeping on both sides, though previously, due to rotator cuff shoulder injuries, I could last but 15 minutes on a side without triggering massive shoulder pain.

If my chronic inflammation could be reduced via enzymes, then why not breast density (and crone's disease's inflammation deposits as well).

Due to this manifest result within my own body, Laura added six weeks of the more aggressive SEFFAFLAZYME to the protocol at the start of the "trust and verify" phase and then added the milder Wobenzyme-N.

Blood Tests

In anticipation of the Doctor Bard visit to visually re-examine the tumor sites via his 3D sonogram, in parallel, I organized two blood tests to uncover any chemical markers indicating on-going cancer activity within Laura's body:

1. another Serum TK test (described earlier) to measure Laura's current degree of internal cell division, and 2), a new test called ONCOBLOT, that looks for unique protein by-products in the blood stream, each made by a specific cancer cell type.

I ordered the Serum TK test kit on-line and had blood drawn locally, and sent it off to the lab.

ONCOBLOT was new, a test made available just recently based upon breakthrough research that isolated certain unique proteins excreted by 26 different cancer cell types. These "marker" proteins, if found floating around in one's bloodstream, indicate cancer activity – breast, lung, colon, etc. - even if tumors are not yet visible. Here is a blog description of ONCOBLOT by a Doctor Chris Foley:

> The best imaging detects cancer only after it has grown to ~ 1 billion cells or more, yet this test can detect cancer that is only 2 million cells large — perhaps months or years before you could see it on a mammogram, colonoscopy, or with a PSA blood test. Maybe there are very less invasive, toxic, or expensive ways to eradicate it long before it becomes a serious illness. "Microscopic cancer" may become a new entity, detected, then eradicated long before a conventional test or worse, symptoms, indicate its presence. Also, if one has had cancer in the past and is being subjected to ongoing scans and tests to detect evidence of recurrence, this could greatly improve the accuracy and reduce radiation exposure.

Laura's long time endocrinologist, Doctor Raffaele in New York - who treated her for thyroid issues - told me about this cutting edge blood test.

After understanding the achievements of ONCOblot Lab's capabilities, Laura and I went to Doctor Raffaele's NYC office and both Laura and myself had blood drawn and sent away to the ONCOblot lab for evaluation (to see if any of the cancer-specific proteins they had in their database matched up with proteins found in our blood samples).

Chapter 20 – Not So Fast

Ok, here comes yet another trip into New York City. This time we went the night before and stayed at the Crown Plaza hotel right in the heart of Times Square. Here is what transpired:

The next morning, our first doctor's appointment began at 9:30 with Doctor Raffaele the endocrinologist, just mentioned, who monitors Laura's biochemical health. This would be followed at 1:30 pm by a Doctor Bard appointment, to scan for visible signs of cancer using his fancy 3D Sonogram and Doppler systems.

Three weeks prior, on our last New York trip, Doctor Raffaele had drawn blood from both Laura and myself and sent the vials to OCONOBLOT to test for traces of cancer. OCONOBLOT, if you recall, only as of 2014, identifies cancer-specific proteins in one's blood serum, with each cancer type releasing its own special protein. So far, OCONOBLOT has identified 26 unique cancer proteins. According to OCONOBLOT, 2 million cancer cells need to be active to output enough measurable protein for this test.

In comparison, visible tumors house from 500 million cells to hundreds of billions, so this cutting edge blood test identifies problems very early on, perhaps years in advance of detecting cancer via mammograms, MRI, PETScans, etc.

Doctor Raffaelle had also sent other blood samples to his regular lab to look into Laura's blood, hormone and vitamin levels.

My ONCOBLOT test came back giving me a clean bill of health, no sign of the 26 cancers lurking in my body.

As expected, Laura's test indicated breast cancer still active.

All of her other numbers across the other blood test were excellent.

Doctor Raffaele, Laura and I mused what to do with this information. If everyone over fifty took the ONCOBLOT test, many hidden cases of cancer would suddenly show, putting many into panic, possibly over nothing.

For example, if one had Colon Cancer proteins in the blood, would that justify injecting chemotherapy into the whole body just to thwart a yet invisible cancer colony?

This level of protein testing certainly opens the door to new treatment dilemmas. Maybe self-healing will be looked at.

In Laura's case, knowing that her body had just killed billions of Breast Cancer cells, the findings meant one thing: give her immune system more time to ferret out the remaining cells; reduce their numbers to a chemically undetectable level.

I propose that anyone taking the OCONOBLOT test and discovering lurking cancer do the same. Use self-healing protocols to reverse the cancer colony's progress long before it can even be seen.

We decided to schedule another ONCOBLOT test six months out.

Ok time for lunch. We walk three blocks to Nello, a top Italian restaurant on Madison Avenue. Laura and I both order salad and Dover Sole, with a bottle of Rose-de-Provence to boot. We had two hours to kill before Doctor Bard.

Lunch was delightful. Unlike a year prior where we shared many a quiet moment, we were quite chatty.

From Nello, another three blocks further east, finds Doctor Bard's office. While sitting in his waiting room he surfaces momentarily and I mention that I have new information.

In the examination room, Doctor Bard goes right to work, setting up for three different scans of Laura's chest cavity and lymph nodes, and he asks me to convey the new information.

I tell him about the two blood tests:

1. RED DROP – which indicates excess or runaway cell division in the body by testing one's TK Serum levels. Cell division in both normal and cancerous cells generates TK; too much TK means more cell division (cancer) than normal.

I said that we had done a few of these RED DROP tests, that Laura's TK numbers were still slightly out of normal range, but had improved drastically over the course of the year as her tumors shrank. This was our *macro* way of gauging Laura's cancer momentum.

2. OCONOBLOT – which tests for specific proteins released by each cancer type, was our *micro* way of gauging Laura's cancer presence. This new test, just available recently, indicated low level Breast Cancer activity somewhere in Laura's body (tissue or lymph glands).

This got the good Doctor going. He concentrated deeply, running his scans, looking for anything evil, finally giving up, and saying that both breasts and all of the lymph nodes looked completely normal. The inert tissue where the large tumor once resided was still there, but identical in condition to where it stood six month's prior: scar tissue with no vascular interaction.

I handed him a piece of paper with *"RED DROP – macro"* and *"OCONOBLOT - micro"* written on it. He went into his office, we to the waiting room.

Minutes went by and Laura asked what was going on. I said that undoubtedly Doctor Bard was on-line looking these tests up.

Sure enough when brought into his office he had already deciphered the claims of both. He did not say they were bogus offerings, but warned that in medicine there are hundreds of break through claims appearing as the next big thing, only to collapse a year out.

I mentioned that with 26 cancer tests to perform, OCONOBLOT found nothing in me, and the correct protein out of 26, for Laura. And that over the past year, Laura's RED DROP TK Serum numbers dropped commensurate with her tumor shrinkage – pretty good evidence that both are viable testing options.

As Doctor Bard has a busy travel schedule, attending many medical conventions, presenting his advanced diagnostic tools, he said he would dig deeper into these tests with colleagues.

But assuming they are valid, he held that Laura's known progress was what counted and with self-healing tools in place we should not consider invasive tactics. We fixed an appointment for six months out.

So what's next? Next was a trip to Georgia and a week of travel baseball competition for our son's Connecticut team. A year prior Laura would not attend such a ridiculous, stressful and fatiguing trip as part of the "no stress" principle, but there was no stopping her this time around. The next day we arrived in 101 degree Atlanta.

Over the next days the topic came up as what to do about squeezing the remaining cancer out. Laura's take was to reinstate the *Infiltration* leg of the protocol. It had been months since she consumed the honey/baking soda concoction and months since ingesting the CBD Oil/Frankincense supplement, as the CBD bottle was dropped and broken, and not re-ordered.

I said fine, we'll get those going, but I found a third infiltration option, *Saffron,* from an article in *Life Extension Magazine.* Saffron, like Frankincense, slows cancer down, with Saffron having three organic molecules that blunt cancer's propensity to divide and multiply.

A week later, the new supplements arrive and *Infiltration* takes the lead role going forward. Now we wait.

Months later in December of 2015, three blood tests are made:

White Blood Cell Nutritional Measurements – to ensure Laura's mineral/vitamin levels were in range.

Red Drop's TK Serum Test – to gauge Laura's cell division level, measured against the general population.

OCONOblot – To detect the microscopic presence of cancer.

Chapter 21 – Digging Even Deeper

It is December of 2015, 19 months since Laura was diagnosed via that original mammogram. The nutrient report comes in looking good, but the Red Drop and OCONOBLOT reports give us pause.

Laura's Red Drop number had not changed from six months prior. The Red Drop ranges are as follows:

20 or Less - Normal Range of TK Activity

21-40 – Moderate TK Activity

41-80 – Pre-Cancerous Levels of TK Activity

81-120 – Risk of Developing Cancer

121 and Over – Active Cancer Range

Laura had a 37, the "Moderate Level", whatever that means. I call Red Drop, and their view is that a steady 37 is nothing to fret about – considering the higher TK levels found when people are consumed by cancer – especially as Laura was twice that level at some point.

Optimism is good – I guess – but I also had the ONCOBLOT report in hand saying that traces of breast cancer were still kicking. And so, though I accepted the encouragement the phone call offered, I knew that a multi-year push was still needed to squash the remaining cancer strong holds.

But still, after all that Laura and I had done over the past 19 months to get this far, I was besides myself as to where the final push would come from.

As it happened, at this very juncture of wonder, my father-in-law Phil, Laura's father, was struggling with diabetes. He was slim, and yet still was in trouble. I decided to look into this for Phil's sake, and I soon stumbled onto an insight that might explain the resolve of Laura's cancer cell holdouts.

A Connection Between Diabetes & Cancer

Earlier in the book I described a sugar absorption test Laura underwent - where a Russian Doctor determined that after a meal, Laura's blood sugar levels remained high for too long.

Since then, Laura moderated her diet to avoid raw sugar and simple carbohydrates, and her big tumors shrank down accordingly.

But the fact that her body holds onto sugar – any sugar – for more than two hours before her cells can fully absorb the incoming supply, still leaves her vulnerable to sugar as follows:

Diabetes, a condition where glucose (sugar) from digested food is not absorbed by the body's cells in a timely manner, results in a build up of sugar in one's blood stream. It is important to understand the causes of diabetes and the fallout of this condition as it pertains, in my opinion, to cancer.

Once the body breaks down incoming food into the "bite-sized" glucose sugar molecules that cells can absorb, the absorption process requires an escort molecule called insulin to bring the glucose to the cell. The insulin molecule is created by the pancreas, which squirts various useful enzymes, including insulin, into the digestive tract, for absorption into the bloodstream.

Once in the blood stream, insulin molecules first bind with glucose molecules – essentially grabbing onto the sugar floating in the blood plasma – and next attach themselves to insulin-specific receptors on cell walls, allowing the cells to take possession of the sugar just brought to them.

When one "has diabetes", either one's pancreas is not making enough of these insulin transporter molecules (Type 1 Diabetes), or over time, one's cell receptors have become insensitive to the insulin molecule and are not binding to it at the needed rate (Type 2 Diabetes).

Or, one could have both conditions in play – insufficient insulin production and enfeebled cell receptors – both the result of genetic weakness, pancreatic infection and/or age. Through either cause, too much sugar effectively corrodes exposed elements of the body's infrastructure – e.g. blood vessels, nerves and skin – leading to conditions like heart disease, blindness and wrinkled bodies.

Whatever the Type 1 or Type 2 combination, with diabetes, trillions of cells are not getting adequate supplies of nutrients.

Large quantities of sugar are simply circulating around in the bloodstream, without landing anywhere – except - at the doorsteps of sugar-starved cancer tumors. Tumor cells have a field day feverously ingesting the sugars to fuel their _anaerobic fermentation of sugar_ method, a method needing 15 times more sugar than the standard _aerobic oxidation of sugar_ followed by non-cancerous cells.

With a cancer situation, any sluggishness by the body in absorbing sugar results in longer sugar-spike durations, thus providing time for tumor cells to "chow down" on their desperately needed levels of sugar.

Though this whole hypothesis needs to be researched, for now, I assume the fact that "diabetes causes sugar duration extension" a factor in provisioning cancer, even when strict with one's diet.

To address this likely situation, Laura added a plant-based supplement called _"Glucose Reduce"_ proscribed by Doctor Brownstein (a holistic M.D.), containing numerous plant extracts known both to provision insulin production inside the pancreas and to promote insulin sensitivity on the cell walls.

To measure the results of this supplement, Laura and I revisited the Russian doctor in Fairfield, Connecticut to measure Laura's sugar duration times before taking the herbal supplement as compared to Laura's "treated" sugar duration time measured 30 minutes after taking the supplement.

First, we ran a baseline metabolic test without taking the supplement to determine Laura's normal metabolism rate. The test starts on an empty stomach. One next drinks sugar water, and over the next two hours the sugar levels in the blood are measured by pricking the finger and finding the blood's sugar level using standard diabetes measurement kits.

In Laura's normal state test, her sugar reading started at 90, rose to 130 and then to 158 and at the two-hour mark ended at 120. Most people's result would have the last reading falling back down around 90, as the ingested sugar would by then be absorbed by the body's muscle cells and organs. In Laura's case, sugar was still circulating.

A week later we ran the same test, but Laura ingested the supplement 30 minutes before drinking the sugar water. This time her final number came down to 95 rather than 120. This showed that the supplement indeed caused the cellular membranes to be more effective in connecting to insulin, able to draw in the circulating sugar at a more standard rate.

The *Glucose Reduce* supplement contains 6-7 herbs known from centuries of traditional medicine to cause this result. I do not know why cellular insulin receptors come alive once in the presence of these herbal compounds, but they obviously do come alive. Anyone with cancer or diabetes should look into the supplement and into experimenting with metabolic testing.

Putting Cancer to Sleep

After pinning down the blood sugar connection to sustaining cancer, I decided to dig into the whole ONCOBLOT phenomena. Who was behind ONCOBLOT, and what else could their inventions teach me? Here is what I found.

How An Organic Compound In Green Tea Blocks The ENOX2 Receptor.

Earlier chapters described the vast chemical operation transpiring inside and outside of the cells, and introduced how "receptors" on cell wall membranes grab onto various organic molecules circulating around the blood stream.

The "keys", the circulating molecules - like nutrients, oxygen, hormones, and enzymes - have specific "lock" receptors that they match up with, opening access to the cell.

Receptor connections serve two macro purposes, first they provide paths into the cell for the raw materials needed to nourish the cell, and second they provide the cell with a communications channel back to the body.

The topic of Green Tea and ENOX2 Receptors is part of the latter, the communications function. NOTE: Incoming communication molecules which couple with receptors – for the purpose of directing cellular behavior - are called "hormones".

Let's first cover hormones. One should realize that the cells of the body do not have minds of their own; instead, hormones govern cellular behavior. Hormones are the way the body directs the cell.

Likewise, cells communicate with the body by releasing their own hormonal beacons, such as distress calls when under duress from hunger and disease. In addition to the receptors designed to deliver nutrients, these specialized receptors focus on the exchange of hormonal signals.

As a reminder, in the *Boosting the Immune System* chapter, a great deal was said about how the various immune agents – T-cells, Antibodies, Macrophages, etc. – coordinate their efforts via hormonal signaling receptors, and how B-cells memorize the receptor shapes of invading viruses, bacteria, funguses and parasites, so that immune cells know how to invade the invaders. The world of receptors seems a vast language of brail-like molecular receptacles looking for their incoming counterpart.

Cell division and programmed cell death – called Mitosis and Apoptosis – is a key communication example of receptor connectivity, where from outside the cell, special incoming hormones direct the cell on what it is to do: *divide or die.*

From everything I have read, no one offers a theory on which cells are told to divide and which cells are told to die. But though there are unknowns in the science of this *divide/die* determination, certain *divide/die* hormonal interactions between the body and the cells have been uncovered in recent years, and these discoveries have led to an understanding of the EONX receptor, the receptor configured receive the *divide/die* hormones.

Many standard receptor designs reside within each cell's DNA library. Cells choose to grow only the receptors they need from the complete inventory: e.g. heart cells have different receptor requirements than do bone cells. When a cell divides, to maintain its cell type, offspring cells reach into the DNA library and switch on the same receptors used by the prior generation

One of the DNA designs, the ENOX gene, holds the blueprint for recognizing incoming *divide/die* hormonal commands. In recent years, it was discovered that the ENOX gene is implemented with either ENOX1 or ENOX2 switch setting options.

Generally, our young cells are born switched to generate ENOX1 receptors, which detect normal cell *division/death* hormonal signals. These normal cells with ENOX1 receptors are able to register *die* signals as well as *grow and divide* signals coming from the body. In one's youth, as cells divide, new cells emerge with these healthy ENOX1 receptors.

Conversely, the "evil" ENOX2 receptor variation appears only on cancer cell walls. This cancer-serving ENOX2 option forms a certain type of receptor that only delivers hormonal signals telling the cell to *grow and divide*.

Because cancer cells only listen to ENOX2 inputs, which solely command *division*, and not to the *die* signals also present in the blood stream, cancer cells are never directed to die.

As a result, like viruses, properly fed cancer cells never die; instead they need to be killed through other means: starvation, poison, radiation, or immune system attacks, etc. ...

As a footnote, one wonders why our bodies formulate the ENOX2 receptor in the first place, as it defies the laws of natural selection.

I suppose that with most cancer deaths occurring past 50 years of age with the "victim" already beyond one's reproductive years, that the destructive ENOX2 trait has already been passed to the next generation long before cancer has taken its toll on the parent. Hence the trait is never weeded out of the population.

So.... We all have to live with this ENOX2 gene sitting within our human DNA library, somewhat like inheriting "original sin" from Adam. Get used to it: we all carry the ability to have our ENOX genes switched to the #2 setting during cell division, when all the switches are set.

What should be done with this new insight?

Recently some smart researchers at Purdue – Doctors James & Dorothy Morre - figured out an *infiltration* scheme that tricks the special ENOX2 receptors into latching onto diversionary molecules, leaving the incoming *grow and divide* hormones no place to land. Thus blocked at the receptor gateway, *grow and divide* signals never reach the cancer cell's nucleus.

And, once the cancer cell is no longer ordered to *grow and divide* by the presence of ENOX2-delivered hormones, the cancer cell just sits there, does nothing, and begins to die of inactivity. With no agenda of its own, only able to react to hormone directives, the cancer cell is effectively put to sleep (permanent sleep).

Ok, I like it! Let's look deeper.

So what diversionary molecule out there fits the bill of matching up with and messing up the degenerate ENOX2 receptacles? The answer: Green Tea molecules!

Actually, the researchers found that by adding a tiny amount of chili pepper to the tea (in a 1:25 ratio), that the match up between cancer cell receptors and the derived tea/pepper compound is quite complete: ENOX2 cancer cell receptors are clogged, smothered, and ultimately denied their precious supply of incoming *grow and divide* hormones.

"Smothering the ENOC2 receptors" is the keystone idea, but there is more to understand about this infiltration tactic against cancer before one tries it out, as follows …

Like any living thing, cancer cells are resourceful. Even if you deprive them for a while, but then "give them an out", just for a short time, they hang tough and live to fight another day.

In this regard, the issue with green tea compounds is two fold: 1) to do the job, one needs to drink 100 cups of tea each day to get enough of the tea's active clogging molecules into one's system, and 2) because the tea molecule is temporary in effect (water soluble) one needs to drink the 100 cups of tea 24/7 to keep the cancer cells smothered at all times. Not happening!

In laboratory tests, cancer cells need to be deprived of ENOX2-delivered hormones for 72 hours before they show signs of surrendering (dying). One should consider a long siege approach with this tactic – say 3 to 6 months in duration. Yet no one can drink 100 cups of tea a day for months on end.

To make this protocol practical, the researchers packaged a high concentration of the green tea/pepper compound into a capsule called CAPSOL-T – each capsule containing 16 cups of the green tea compound, with only slight traces of caffeine. These are taken every four hours.

To bridge the eight-hour sleep gap, a "slow release" sister capsule called CAPSOL-TSR disperses the compound over eight hours. Nice job!

In one clinical test 40 individuals who tested positive for traces of cancer using the OCONOblot test (described in an earlier chapter), followed the tea protocol, with 38 of 40 ultimately obtaining clean OCONOblot test results.

A second footnote goes back to my theory on the root cause of cancer: that viruses sometimes modify normal cells during cell division. Yet according to ENOX2 findings, the virus may only need to influence a switch, not the whole cell – like having the new cell become an ENOX2 receptor cell rather than an ENOX1 receptor cell. The newly made cancer cell then grows ENOX2 receptors on its membrane wall, not a big deal, since this is an option within its DNA library.

That a simple genetic switch setting can make a newly divided cell impervious to 'die" signals, without destabilizing the cells overall makeup, makes formation of cancer in this manner a way less mysterious phenomenon than alternative explanations - like "spontaneous mutation" of the DNA itself.

Hence colon cells remain colon cells but with ENOX2 receptors, breast cells stay breast cells but now grow ENOX2 receptors, and so forth across the 100 types of cancer cells known to science.

BTW, the patented OCONOblot test itself (also invented by the Morre's) works by dissecting the ENOX2 discharges released by cancer cell receptors into the blood serum, as follows.

Although all cancers emit traces of the ENOX2 receptor into the blood serum, each cancer cell type slightly modifies the ENOX2 receptor at the molecular level, leaving a signature marker behind for each cancer type. This is used by the testing lab to categorize the cancer as breast, lung, colon, etc.

Finally, though green tea is ingested daily in the *Orient* at much lower concentrations then the green tea/pepper supplement capsules, it manifestly works to some degree in the general population, as the incidences of cancer in green tea drinking cultures is notably less than in those cultures not following the practice (the same with chili pepper eaters).

And recall, that besides the receptor-blocking benefits of green tea, other benefits, like anti-oxidant support (described in a previous chapter), are included on the "Green Tea Menu".

What do these combined Green Tea/ENOX findings add up to?

So far the cancer defeating protocol outlined in this book calls for a) starving cancer via *Diet*, i.e. depriving it of sugar, b) by *Empowerment, i.e.* boosting the body via detoxification, oxygen and energy enhancement and with special nutrient supplements that fortify immune cells, and c) via *Infiltration*, i.e. infusing cancer with poisons like Frankincense, Saffron and Baking Soda, making the cells weak.

But here, with green tea, we add a new *Infiltration* tactic; we put the cancer cell to sleep. I like it. A lot!

The End – For Now

So today, in 2018 we continue with much of the protocol, though more fruit sugar and carbs are consumed along with wine than in the "total war" months of year one. Laura usually remembers to take a glucose reduce pill before a meal and pretends that granola with honey is fine.

But considering her excellent health markers and constant energy level, we let her habits stay as they are. We take this tactic knowing that Dr. Bard's detailed 3-D sonogram technology can scour Laura's whole chest cavity every six months, able to spot the slightest sign of cellular aberration.

In 2017 Laura's good health continued, with another good sonogram report in November 2017. And, as I seemed not to be uncovering key new insights, felt it time to publish this book – updated editions to come out in due course.

Epilogue

One day, when my first wife was doing well on the macrobiotic "Japanese" diet, I described it to a Russian cab driver in New York City, and he exploded, actually taking his hands off of the wheel, proclaiming…

What is for life? You eat. You sleep. You make love. You die!

He went on to say that he neither supported the macrobiotic diet nor medical intervention. His view: *When your time is up, it's up!* And I know two people of high character who were diagnosed with cancer that elected to do nothing. They quickly died – in 90-days time - without a lot of fanfare.

And so, I do not claim that everything you have just read is the way forward or the whole truth; I just know that some combination of the inscribed ideas and actions, *The Self-Healing Protocol*, worked for Laura, the mother of our four children.

Aspects of Medical Intervention also work, yet these doctors do not necessarily know the whole truth either. Keep in mind that traditional doctors, backed by positive five-year statistics, actually advocate treatment approaches that attack every cell in the body. I simply cannot get over this fact, and, admittedly, I hold it against them.

I am prejudiced. In the past, with my first wife, in the cancer wards of the finest hospitals in New York for over a ten-year period, I saw the intense suffering of patients enduring surgery and body poisoning, believing they were somehow noble, fighting cancer.

They were fighting treatment.

The possibility of empowering the body - as a first step towards arresting cancer - was never mentioned. Many a doctor told me that there was no evidence that sugar drives cancer, and many believed that vitamins did drive cancer. In the hospital the patient was served sweet deserts and no vitamins.

I know of cases where a large tumor was found, and in preparation for eventual surgery, the patient given 8 weeks of radiation and some chemo to shrink the tumor.

Once the tumor was knocked down a bit, surgery was scheduled for 10-12 weeks out.

Before the surgery date 20 weeks went by, with no interim attempt made to enlist the body via self-healing to further shrink the cancer.

Had one been following elements of *The Self-Healing Protocol* during this prep round of radiation/chemo in the months leading up to surgery, the patient could safely experiment with various diet, detoxification and infiltration tactics.

If the tumor shrank further than expected, then great - one buys more time for *Self-Healing*, delaying surgery and placing the patient in the driver's seat.

In some way, medical intervention, by ignoring the body's potential to prevail, embraces the disease without "push back", wrestling the disease on the disease's terms. The cancer is killed by surgery, radiation and chemotherapy, but the body is not fortified, so the cancer can reform to fight another day.

The disease's powerful medical institutional allies keep Cancer-Killing strategies in the forefront. Promising young and impressionable minds attend medical school. Some decide to specialize in cancer. Some of these then specialize in oncology, radiation or surgery. Some of these then specialize in tumor versus blood cancer...

But ultimately they choose a practice where either they cut, burn or poison flesh, believing they are experts at curing cancer.

No, they are experts at killing cancer accepting high levels of collateral damage – like breaking 1,000 eggs to make a small omelet.

And once in the mode of killing cancer, statistics formulated across large populations of patients can be gathered – clinical evidence – to determine effectiveness. Yes, when proposing *alien drugs, severe surgery or repeated radiation*, backed up by clinical evidence across populations, there seems no other choice.

Conversely, with *Self Healing*, the evidence one looks for is strictly within oneself. Have I got the body working? Are the tumors shrinking? If not, consider invasive tactics.

It is a different kind of truth – a singular, personal truth of the resilience of one's particular body to fight rouge cancer cells. *Self-Healing* sits outside the universe of intervention risks, statistics and probabilities. It is something specific to you, certain detail that you can monitor.

Finally, compare what you have just read in this book to the autocratic proclamations of the top *Medical Intervention* institutions, and come to your own conclusion on which approach resides closer to the "Truth." Here they are:

Mayo Clinic - *Researchers have identified factors that can increase your risk of breast cancer. But it remains unclear why some people who have no risk factors still develop cancer, yet other people with risk factors never do. It's likely that a complex interaction of one's genetic makeup and your environment causes breast cancer.*

American Cancer Society - *Many risk factors can increase your chance of developing breast cancer, but we do not yet know exactly how some of these risk factors cause cells to become cancerous. Certain changes (mutations) in DNA that "turn on" cell division or "turn off" tumor suppressor genes can cause normal breast cells to become cancerous. At this time, the best advice to possibly reduce the risk of breast cancer remains to:*

Get regular, intentional physical activity.

Reduce your lifetime weight gain by limiting your calories and getting regular physical activity.

Avoid or limit your alcohol intake.

National Breast Cancer Foundation *- No one knows the exact causes of breast cancer. Doctors seldom know why one woman develops breast cancer and another doesn't, and most women who have breast cancer will never be able to pinpoint an exact cause. What we do know is that breast cancer is always caused by damage to a cell's DNA.*

As said, I assume that there are flaws and missing elements to *The Self-Healing Protocol*, but I'd take it *as is,* any day, next to the *Medical Industrial Complex* of Researchers, Practitioners, Hospitals, Specialists, Charities, Insurance Companies, Insurance Regulators, Drug Companies and the FDA – all embracing a statistically-driven approach to killing cancer from the outside, rather than provisioning the body from the inside.

Doing your own thing is not sacrilegious; it is self-evident.

Loose Ends

In the course of four-years of research I read other cancer theorists who operated outside of mainstream medicine. Two include Doctor Max Gerson (1881 – 1959) and Doctor Nickolas Gonzales (1947 - 2015). In common, both believed in cleaning up embedded toxins – advocating coffee enemas to draw toxins out – and both taught the use of diet to fortify the body's own defensive mechanisms. One should look into their protocols, even just to gauge the range of theoretical possibilities.

Doctor Gonzales, notably, analyzed illness from the vantage point of how one's weakened nervous system debilitates the body's core organs and functions. I read his book *Nutrition and the Anatomic Nervous System*, and it spoke to some of the open questions I pondered.

It seems self-evident that nervous system imperfections inhibit the body's cancer fighting abilities, though the nervous system/ cancer connection is rarely considered. Let's sketch out the nervous system basics, and how it meshes with some of my loose ends – including: *tumor versus blood cancers, insomnia, autoimmune conditions, diabetes, and the use of enzymes to thwart cancer.*

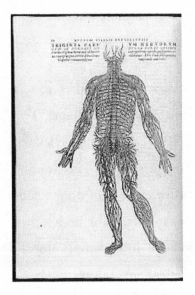

Recall, that although earlier I mentioned the body's *active awake* and *restful sleep* states - saying how we channeled Laura away from stress and towards rest - I did not go deeper into the nervous system's architecture (left). Understanding how this invisible 200-billion cell communication network operates will provide food-for-thought on my "loose end" subjects. Here goes.

To start, one can visualize the nervous system as a) an *outward facing* enterprise that *vividly* channels incoming sensory data – sight, smell, sound, feel, taste - through the thalamus into the cerebral cortex, where judgmental decisions are made, and b) an *internal facing* enterprise called the anatomic nervous system, that *quietly* monitors the inner workings of the body – heart, lung, blood pressure, digestive track dynamics – all without our being aware of it.

The outward facing sensory enterprise is easier to grasp, as we actually experience it continually. But the internal, anatomic system is quite stealth, as it operates without our awareness of it.

And just as there are two circulatory systems – blood and lymph, there are two internal anatomic nervous systems: the active awake set, referred to as the *sympathetic* system, and the restful sleep set called the *parasympathetic* system. The fact that two complete sets of nerves are feathered amongst our universe of cells is – amazing!

When one is awake and on the go, the sympathetic system dominates, firing electrical impulses throughout the body driving the offensive organs like the brain and heart, causing action-oriented hormonal releases – such as cortisol.

Conversely, when it's time to eat or sleep, the sympathetic unit backs down and the parasympathetic nerves take over, firing electrical impulses that amongst other things, cause one's digestive track to engage and one's immune system to come alive.

These two physical nervous systems use electrical signals and hormone triggers to prod and temper the various body parts to perform their functions.

Sitting above the anatomic networks, an amazing air traffic controller operates called the *hypothalamus* – the size of an almond; it coordinates the 3-way interplay between sympathetic and parasympathetic activity, and the body's hormonal glands.

The hypothalamus resides at the base of the scull, attached to the spinal cord. It receives sensory input from the cerebral cortex while simultaneously monitoring the sympathetic and parasympathetic signaling coming in from the internal organs of the body. Busy, busy!

I am in awe that so much is deciphered by this tiny "thing", the hypothalamus. Did evolution - random mutations - cause this brilliant coordinator that lives within every animal species?

Besides monitoring heart rate and water retention, the hypothalamus interacts in concert with the brain, recognizing the "danger" and "safe" circumstances one experiences out in the world. These real-time, danger/safe moments are gleaned by the always-alert hypothalamus as it "listens" to mood signals flowing down the spinal cord from the cerebral cortex.

To determine danger versus safety, the cerebral cortex digests sensations coming in from the five senses and determines the disposition of these as dangerous (stressful) or safe (calming), thus setting the mood, which it broadcasts down the spinal cord. The hypothalamus monitors these signals and reacts to them. How?

Sitting beneath the hypothalamus is the pea-sized *pituitary gland* that releases many different hormones into the blood stream based upon marching orders coming from the hypothalamus gland.

For example, if a dog chases you, the senses report data to the thalamus and the cerebral cortex, which recognizes trouble. The diligent hypothalamus, picking up on the *danger/stress* vibe, triggers the sympathetic nerves to fire up, and it releases a sympathetic-command to the pituitary gland which immediately sends out an "all-hands-on-deck" hormone to downstream glands.

Based upon sympathetic nerve firings and the pituitary hormones, cortisol, for instance, is made by the adrenal glands, further spurring on the heart and other muscles to get pumping.

Likewise, when the sun goes down, the cerebral cortex recognizes that it is closing in on bed time. This *calm* vibe is picked up by the hypothalamus, which bumps up the parasympathetic system, and commands the pituitary gland to release parasympathetic hormones – like melatonin - throughout the body, waking up the immune system. The immune system stays active so long as the parasympathetic system is firing away.

Interesting, but how does this relate to our health?

According to Doctor Gonzales, different people have variations on how well this whole mechanism works. Some people have strong sympathetic systems which over-dominate their bodies, some have a balance between the two sets of nerves, and some people have overly-dominant parasympathetic systems.

But even if balanced, both systems may be either strong or weak, or both may be over-firing concurrently (anxiety), so we are all vulnerable to how well the hypothalamus directs our bodies on a 24/7 basis - for life. One can imagine the long range effect on the body when the systems are unbalanced or weak.

Of course, the hypothalamus could be doing fine, but the downstream glands, like the adrenal's, could be failing. Diagnostics is complex.

Here is the rub. Doctor Gonzales theorized that sympathetic dominant bodies are prone to develop *tumor cancers*, because parasympathetic dependent organs like the pancreas are stifled via neglect, depriving the body of key pancreatic enzymes needed to thwart blooming cancer cells.

Parasympathetic dominant bodies cause the opposite. They are prone to *blood cancers* like leukemia, as the runaway parasympathetic state overheats the immune system, causing proliferating and mutating stem cells in the bone marrow.

Gonzales' protocol sought to bring balance, vitality and order to both systems, thus avoiding the cancer pitfall of either extreme, while also tempering anxiety and depression caused by both systems firing in conflict.

In summary, sympathetic dominant bodies need vegetables, magnesium and potassium to strengthen the weak parasympathetic side, and parasympathetic dominant bodies need plenty of meat and calcium to build up the weaker sympathetic side of the overall mechanism.

Doctor Gonzales was controversial not for the architectural basics described above, but because he believed that anti-cancer pancreatic enzymes could cure tumor cancer if present in the blood steam at an ample concentration. To achieve this, he advocated strengthening the parasympathetic side via a vegetarian diet, vitamin/mineral supplements, and intravenous supplementation of the pancreatic enzyme itself.

In one comparison test of terminally ill patients the Gonzales patients died before the chemotherapy patients, yet all died. Critics dismissed the whole "enzyme" concept, though Gonzales had results with many cancer cases.

Previously in the book, I mentioned enzyme therapy, saying we passed on it, and the above explains the back story to this decision. The fact that Doctor Gonzales died in 2015, prior to me contacting him, left no one to enlighten me further. None of that, though, offsets the basic physiology of wanting a balanced and strong sympathetic/parasympathetic system. This knowledge is pivotal.

Also earlier in this book I wondered if Laura's dietary protocol worked only with tumor-based cancers. According to anatomic theory, the answer is yes ... tumor cancers require raw and cooked vegetables to build up the parasympathetic side, boosting the organs and the immune cells. Blood cancers require an opposite protocol, needing the amino acids brought in from meat – though sugar and carbs are out for both, and a detoxed body is the starting point for both ends of the spectrum.

Other topics to ponder.

In addition, by just contemplating the structure of the anatomic nervous system, I speculate that insomnia exists when the sympathetic side fires endlessly, overwhelming attempts by the parasympathetic side to shut the body down. Hence Laura's hot salt baths at night empirically shifted her anatomic balance towards *restful sleep*.

More, I wonder if autoimmune conditions are spurred on by a dominant parasympathetic side which endlessly drives the immune cells to find and destroy targets. If so, a build up one's sympathetic side which will rest the immune system, might naturally interrupt auto-immune flare-ups.

Also, regarding diabetes type 1 - low insulin -, this condition could be affected by an anatomic imbalance which, again, deprives the pancreas (which makes insulin) of adequate parasympathetic stimulus. Hypothalamus issues could also drive type 2 diabetes – the sluggishness of cells to grab onto glucose-laden insulin molecules. With type 2, the liver and muscle cells deprived of adequate parasympathetic stimulus might simply stay lethargic.

One more thing. At some point, I looked into the phenomenon of the different human blood types, hoping to glean an insight, but only found the following. Overall, before modern times humans lived within broad biospheres – like the fertile crescent, jungles, frozen northlands, etc. …, eating only the food found in their cloistered world.

A meat and milk eating Mongol evolved a different internal system than did a grain-producing Egyptian.

But then two things happened: First, to some extent, the races interbred so that today's integrated gene pool may contain *conflicted traits*. Second, our food today has nothing to do with a specialized biosphere – we grow and eat what we want.

Our bodies cope with this imposed "modern" chaos, but when the body breaks down, rather than knee-jerk medical intervention, the person involved has a possibility to slowly align their diet to their genetic preferences, pulling the the combined sets of digestive and anatomic nervous systems back in line.

These loose ends, of course, are but educated, correlated guesses. But like everything else human, one starts with a contemplated premises and then tries things out. Where are the young researchers?

I will leave you with that.

CPSIA information can be obtained
at www.ICGtesting.com
Printed in the USA
BVOW08s1418290318
511908BV00001B/2/P